WINDON · MARLBOROUGH · CH
CRICKLADE · HIGHW

'T

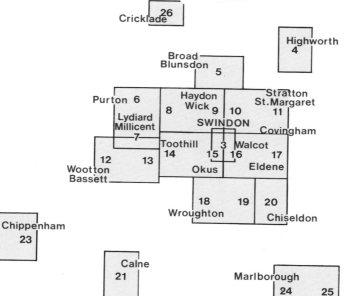

Cricklade 26

Highworth 4

Broad Blunsdon 5

Purton 6

Haydon Wick 9 · 10

Stratton St.Margaret 11

Lydiard Millicent 7

8

SWINDON

Covingham

Toothill 14

Wootton Bassett

12   13

3 Walcot

15 16   17

Okus

Eldene

18   19   20

Wroughton

Chiseldon

Chippenham

22   23

Calne

21

Marlborough

24   25

Every effort has been made to verify the accuracy of information in this book but the publishers cannot accept responsibility for expense or loss caused by any error or omission. Information that will be of assistance to the user of the maps will be welcomed.

The representation of a road, track or footpath on the maps in this atlas is no evidence of the existence of a right of way.

One-way Street	→
Car Park	℗
Place of Worship	✦
Post Office	●
Public Convenience	⒞
Pedestrianized	▨

Scale of street plans: 4 inches to 1 mile
Unless otherwise stated

Street plans prepared and published by ESTATE PUBLICATIONS, Bridewell House, TENTERDEN, KENT, and based upon the ORDNANCE SURVEY mapping with the permission of The Controller of H. M. Stationery Office.

The publishers acknowledge the co-operation of the local authorities of towns represented in this atlas.

Estate Publications 209 H   ISBN 0 86084 808 6   © Crown Copyright 398713

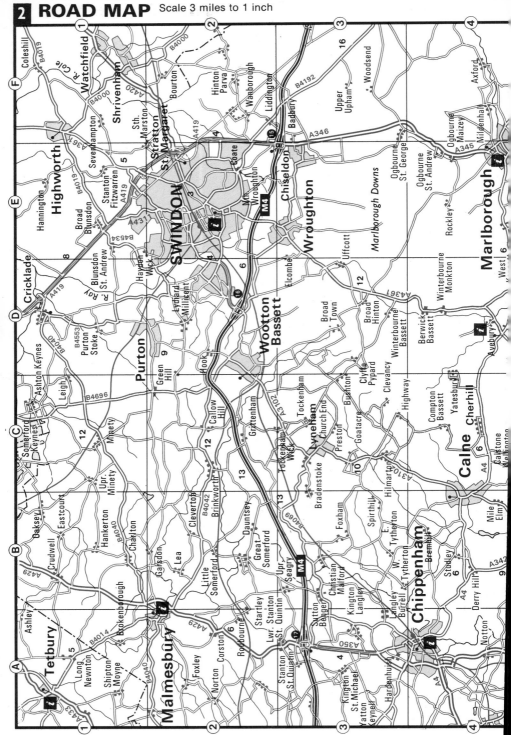

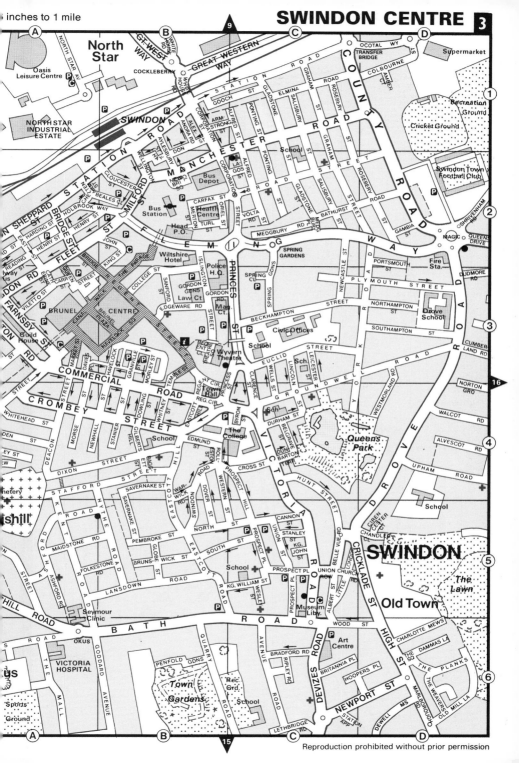

4 HIGHWORTH

The Briary

Everslea

BLACKWORTH INDUSTRIAL ESTATE

Sewage Works

Haresfield

A361

PENTLANDS LANE

CRANE FURLONG

DRIVE

ROUND HILLS MEAD

SEVENFIELDS

EDEN CROFT

KNOWLANDS

WESSEX WAY

Common Farm

SKYE RD
KILDA
ARRAN CT
WAY
MICHAELS CRES
GROVE ORCHARD
AVENUE
POUND
BROOKFIELD
PENTLA
SON CL
GROVE HILL
HENLEY
FOLLY CRES
FOLLY DRI
FOLLY CL
WEST

Northview County Prim. Sch.

THE DORMERS

QUEENS AV

VORDA RD

THE CULLERNS

THE DORMERS

SPA CLOSE

LISMORE RD
STROMA
WY
BUTE CL
ISLAY CL
BARRA CL
HOME FARM
PRIM. School
WESTROP
WESTROP
NEWBURGH PL
RIVERS PL
QUART CRT
HAINE
MIDDI
HAINE
DOWNS VW
QUEENS AV
ORANGE CL
CHERRY ORCHARD
THE CULLERNS
PRIORY
THE CULLERNS
BIDDEL SPRINGS
PRIORY GRN
ROUND HILLS MEAD

Police Station

Home Farm
STATION RD
STAPLETON CL
CHURCH
ST MICHAELS
WINDRUSH
NORTH
AVENUE
W
CHERRY CL
CHERRY CL
VICARAGE LA
THE MEWS
SHEEP ST
MKT PL
HIGH ST
PARSONAGE CT
PRIORY GRN
ERI GRN
ERI GRN
THE WILLOWS

Hampton Hill

OAK DRI

BLOE MILL GDNS

Cemetery

CRICKLADE
ROAD
B4019

BOTANY
ROMAN WAY
WRDE HILL
WESTVI CL
THE ELMS
TENNIS Courts
Swim. Pool
Recreation Ground
Pav.
Pav.
Bowling Green

SWINDON ST
BREWERY ST
EASTROP

Liby

Libby

BLAND FORD ALLEY

KINGS
THE BROOKS
ORANGE GRN
Sch
School
PARK AV
KINGS AV

Eastrop Grange

Highworth

Botany

Golf
Course

SWINDON ROAD

STONE FIELDS

Warneford School

SHRIVENHAM ROAD

Golf Course

The Buildings

Redland Court

A361

Redlands

ROAD

Wrag Cottage

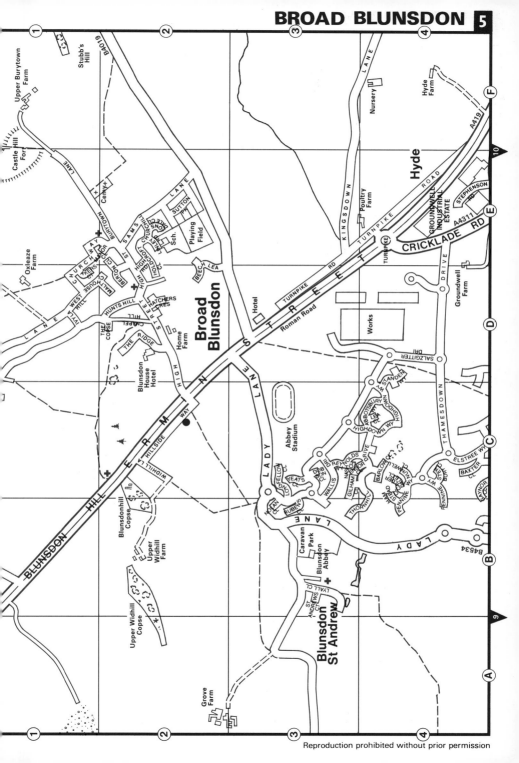

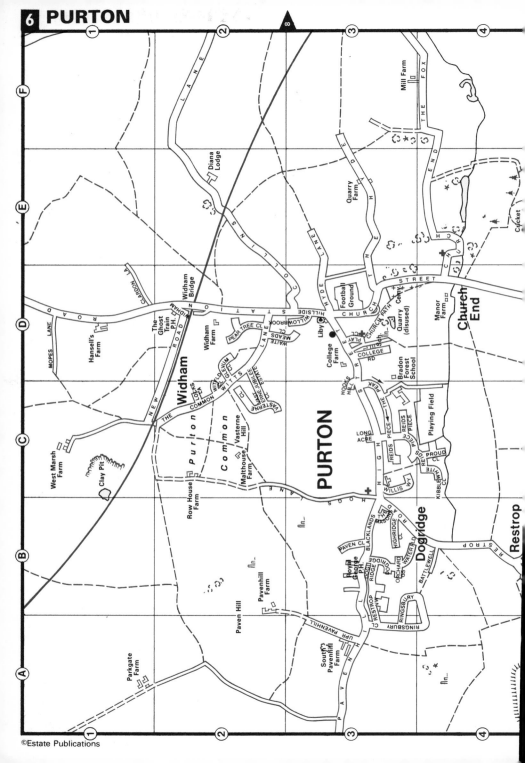

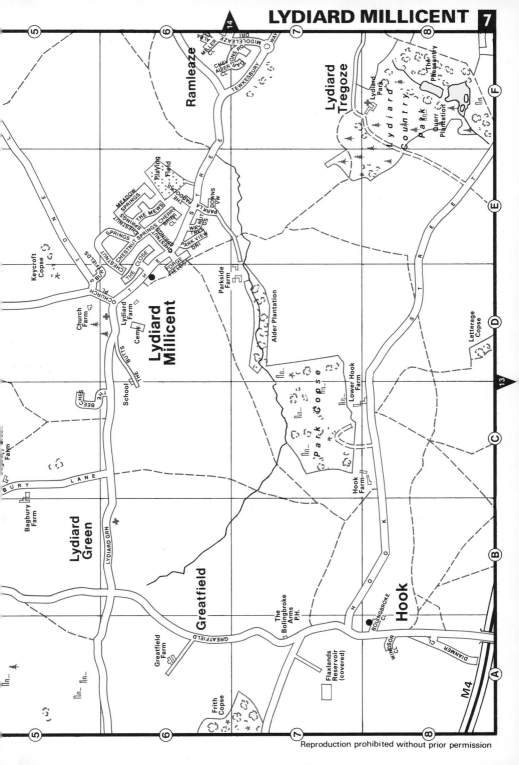

B4553

Pry Farm

The Pry

COLLINS LANE

Pry Holding

Bremhill Bridge

Oil Storage Depot

Mill Farm

Bremhill Farm

Purton Mill

Ridgeway Farm

Stone House Farm

STONE LANE

Bridys

THE CRES

P U R T O N

Westhills Lodge

Selbrook House

Nine Elms

THE CRES

FURZE CL

CLAYHILL

HORSELL

CHASE

INLEY

HIGHMOOR

SWINLEY DRI

RUSSELL

COMP CEN

Comp Cen

Peatmoor Copse

FIREBOX HILL

WINTER

Health Centre

Lake

WEB

LETTERAGE

WOOD

SOUND COPSE

HARDCOT

RANNOCH

MELFORT

SANDAL

Peatmoor

MARDALE

KINGS

DRI

SANDACRE RD

BISHOP

RIDGCOT

YARNTON

BILLYD

OLD FORD

OASTHOUSE

CARGRAVE

THE

VESTER

LANGLEY

MIDDLELEAZE DRI

CERNE

PILTON

OLD SHAW LA

ROUGH MOOR

CARTWRIGHT

BAIRD

OLD SHAW LA

Shaw

Haydon

Oakhurst

Guernsey Farm

Haydon End Farm

Haydon Farm

Park Co

Nursery

R. Ray

ROSEMARY RD

CORIANDER CL

PARSLEY

SAGE CL

BORAGE

BAY LEAF AV

FENNEL AV

BRYONY

CLARY RD

MARJORAM

CHIVES

MINT CL

NUTMEG

BASIL CL

SCL

JASM

KEY
MOU.

SORRE

SOUTHERNWOOD DRI

TARRAGON DRI

CAYENNE

CARRAWAY

WEST FIELD

WOOD HALL

WINKLE CL

CHICORY

THYME CL

PURTON RD

WOOD HALL

BAKERS

PURTON

ELBOROUGH

Elborough Bridge

THAMESDOWN DRIVE

ROAD

NESS

BURLING

KESTREL

SPARCE

LOWES

MELFORT

SOUND COPSE

SANDOWN

Sparcells

Hreod Parkway School

Outfall

Outfall

HILLMEAD

MARSHALL

DRIVE

WAY

MEAD

WAY

PEATMOOR

BISHOP

HILLMEAD

HILLMEAD EMPLOYMENT AREA

Sch. MA

KEY

HEATH

CARES DRI

RIVERMEAD

VISA

DRIVE

Sludge Beds

Filter & Pump Ho.

Sewage Works Pump H

Filter Bed

Tar

A B C D

1 2 3 6 4 5 6

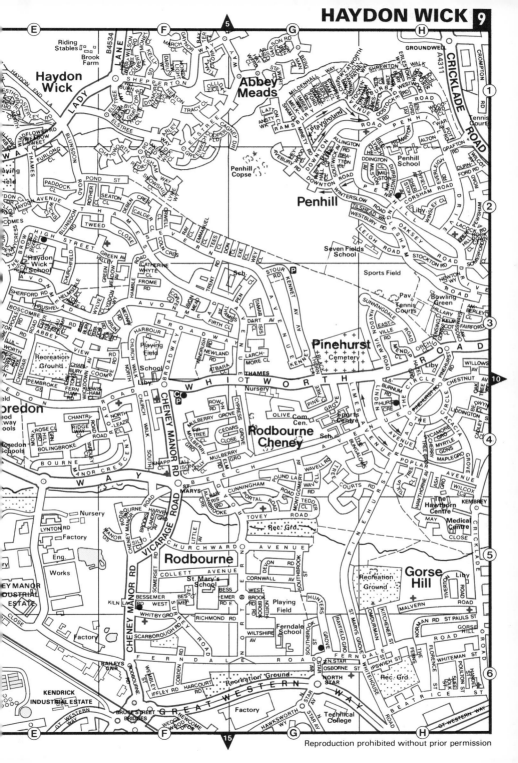

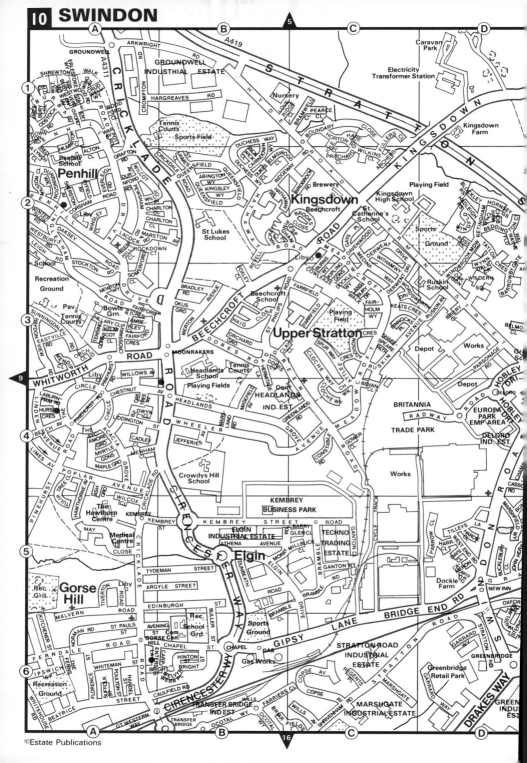

STRATTON ST MARGARET

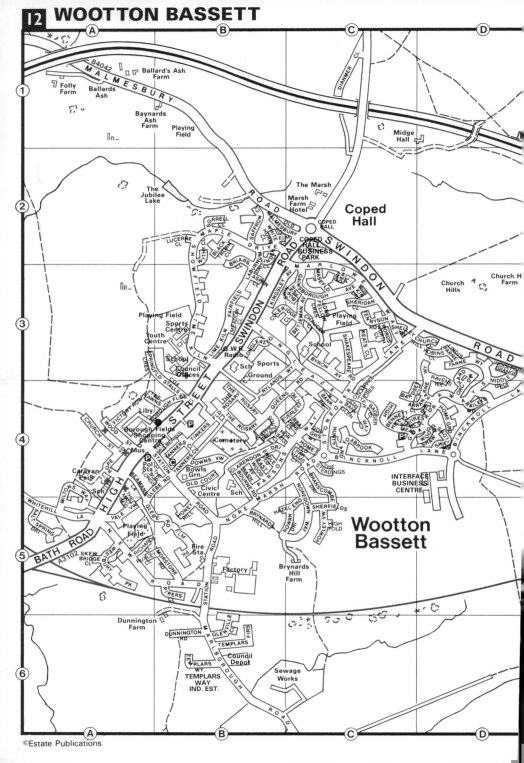

12 WOOTTON BASSETT

Wootton Bassett

Coped Hall

©Estate Publications

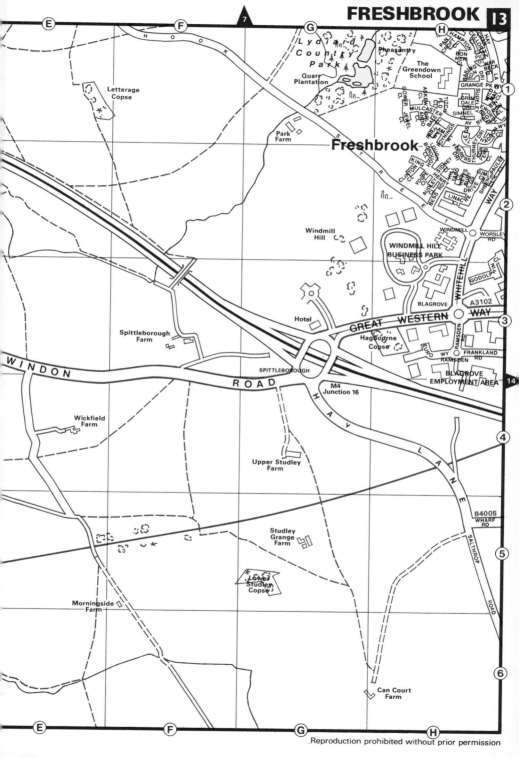

7

Freshbrook

Lydiard Country Park

Pheasantry

The Greendown School

Quarr Plantation

Letterage Copse

Park Farm

Windmill Hill

WINDMILL HILL BUSINESS PARK

Windmill

WORSLEY RD

GODOLPH.. CL

BLAGROVE

A3102

Hotel

GREAT WESTERN WAY

Hagbourne Copse

SPITTLEBOROUGH

Spittleborough Farm

EURO WY

RAMSDEN

FRANKLAND RD

BLAGROVE EMPLOYMENT AREA

WINDON ROAD

M4 Junction 16

HAY LANE

Wickfield Farm

Upper Studley Farm

Studley Grange Farm

Lower Studley Copse

Morningside Farm

B4005 WHARF RD

SALTHROP ROAD

Can Court Farm

14

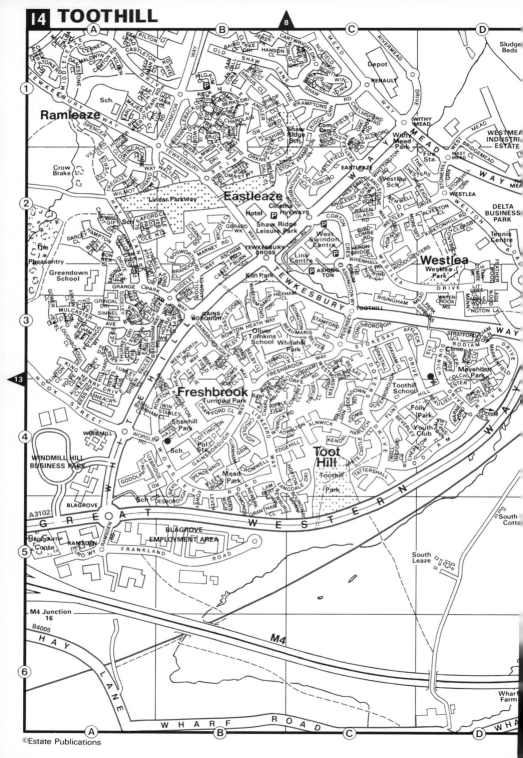

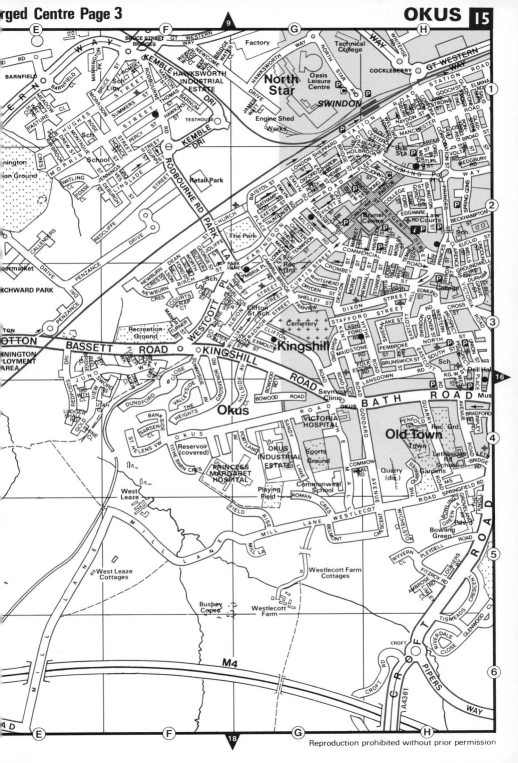

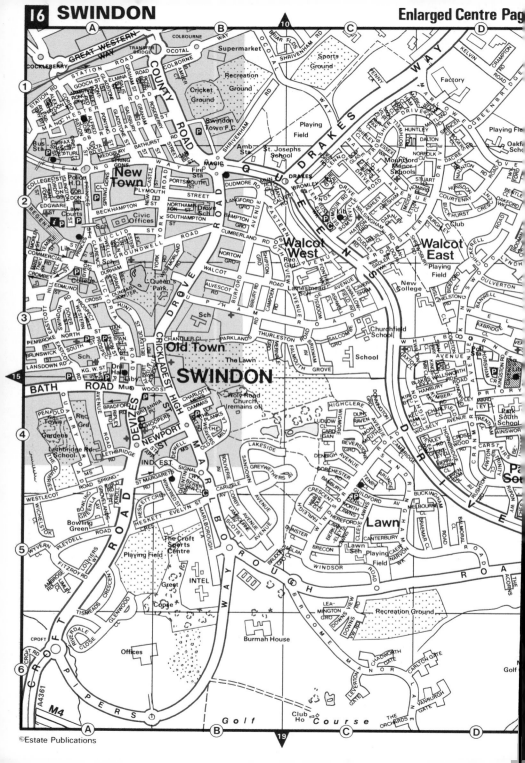

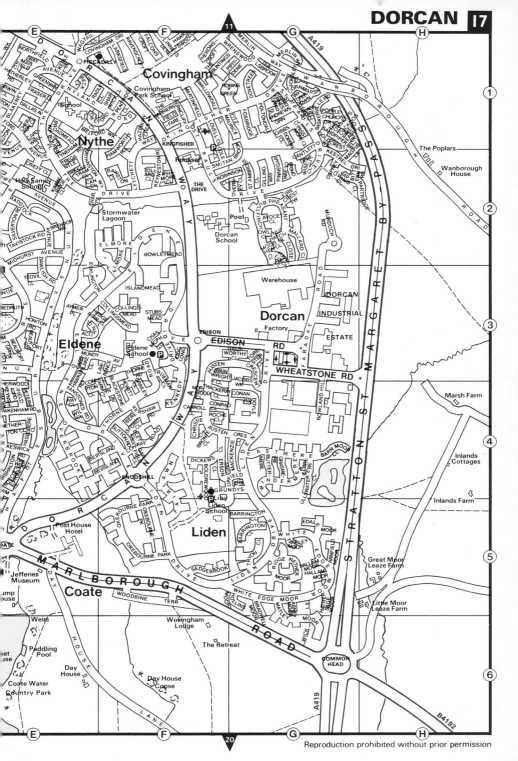

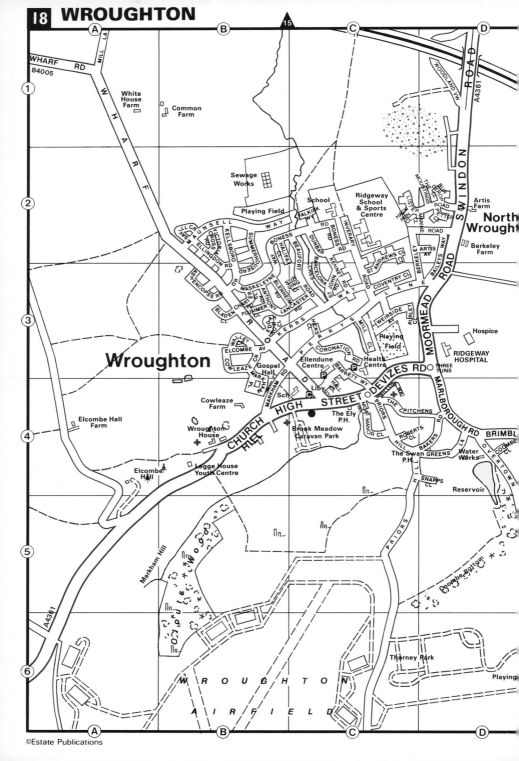

WHARF RD
B4005

MILL LA

WHARF

White House Farm

Common Farm

Sewage Works

Playing Field

School

Ridgeway School & Sports Centre

FALKIRK WY

WAY

North Wrought

Artis Farm

Berkeley Farm

CRUNSELL
VICTORA CROSS
KELLSBORO RD
ELLINGDON RD
SUMMERHOU
MASKELEYNE WY
ANTHONY
BLENHEIM
BONESS
HALIFAX
BEAUFORT
DUNBAR
BARCELONA
PRESTON RD
KENNET RD
INVERARY
BONESS RD
RD

St ANDREWS CL
COVENTRY CL

BERKELEY AV
ARTIS AV

BAILEYS WY

SWINDON ROAD

A4361

WOODLAND VW

ROAD

MOORMEAD

Wroughton

SPENCOPSE RD
BLADEN
PLUMMER
CR
CHURCH
ELDENE
TERRS

MASK HY

KING RD
LANCASTER
PERRY'S
MILL

WALLEY CR
ELCOMBE AV
COWLEAZE

ELCOMBE
GOSPEL HALL

MARKHAM RD

PE

CORONATION RD

ELLENDUNE CENTRE

Health Centre

Playing Field

WEIRSIDE AV
PURLEY
LANE

Hospice

RIDGEWAY HOSPITAL

THREE TUNS

DEVIZES RD

Cowleaze Farm

Elcombe Hall Farm

Wroughton House

Legge House Youth Centre

Elcombe Hall

Library
Sch

HIGH STREET

CHURCH HILL

Brook Meadow Caravan Park

The Ely P.H.

The Swan P.H.

BARRETT WY
NIGHT MANOR CL
ROBERTS CL
BAKERS
HILL
SNAPPS CL

PRIORS HILL

THE PITCHENS

GREENS LA

MARLBOROUGH RD

Water Works

Reservoir

BRIMBL
COOMBE
OVERTOWN

Markham Hill

WROUGHTON WOODS

Coombe Bottom

WROUGHTON AIRFIELD

Thorney Park

Playing

A4361

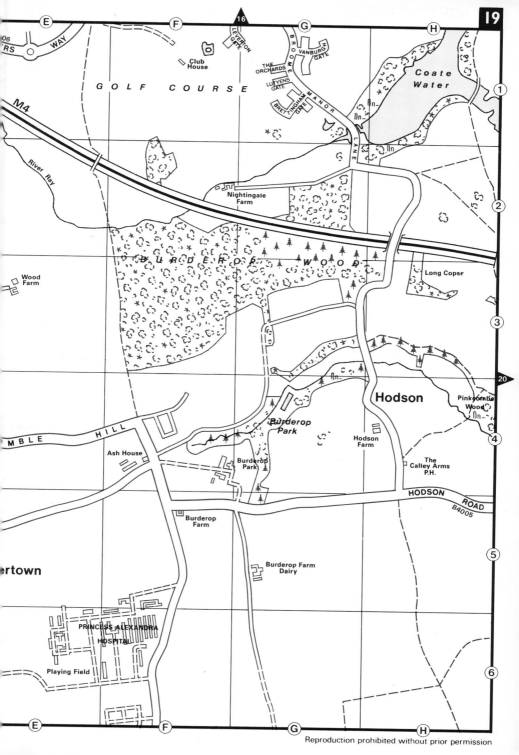

E   F   16   G   H

Club House

GOLF COURSE

LEVERTON GATE

BROOME

VANBURG GATE

THE ORCHARDS

LUTYENS GATE

BRETYINGHAM GATE

MANOR LANE

Coate Water

①

M4

River Ray

Nightingale Farm

②

Wood Farm

BURDEROP WOOD

Long Copse

③

20

Hodson

Pinkcombe Wood

MBLE HILL

Ash House

Burderop Park

Hodson Farm

The Calley Arms P.H.

④

Burderop Park

HODSON ROAD B4005

Burderop Farm

⑤

Burderop Farm Dairy

rtown

PRINCESS ALEXANDRA HOSPITAL

Playing Field

⑥

E   F   G   H

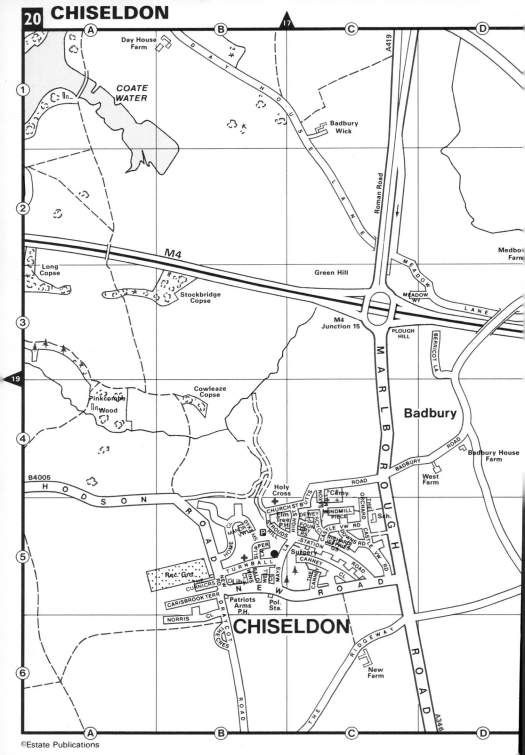

COATE WATER

Day House Farm

Badbury Wick

A419

Roman Road

MEADOW WY

MEADOW LANE

Medbo Farm

M4

Green Hill

Long Copse

Stockbridge Copse

M4 Junction 15

PLOUGH HILL

BERRICOT LA

19

Cowleaze Copse

Pinkcombe Wood

MARLBOROUGH ROAD

Badbury

ROAD

BADBURY ROAD

West Farm

Badbury House Farm

B4005

HODSON ROAD

Holy Cross

CHURCH ST

Elm Tree P.H.

DEWEY

WINDMILL PIECE

Cerny.

ORCHARD

THE

Sch.

HIGH ST

BUTTS

DOWNS RD

CASTLE VW RD

DIKES

HOME CL

MANOR

P

STROUDS HILL

FOUN DRY

CASTLE

STATION RD

HIPPARD JEFFRIES

CANNEY

Rec. Grnd.

CURNICRS

TURNBALL

NEW

SLIPPER

MAYS

Liby.

BALDS

WINS

WEB

LA

Surgery

THE CANNEY

CL

CASTLE VW RD

CARISBROOK TERR

NORRIS CL

DRAYCOT CRES

Patriots Arms P.H.

Pol. Sta.

NEW ROAD

CHISELDON

RIDGEWAY

THE

ROAD

A346

New Farm

DAY HOUSE LANE

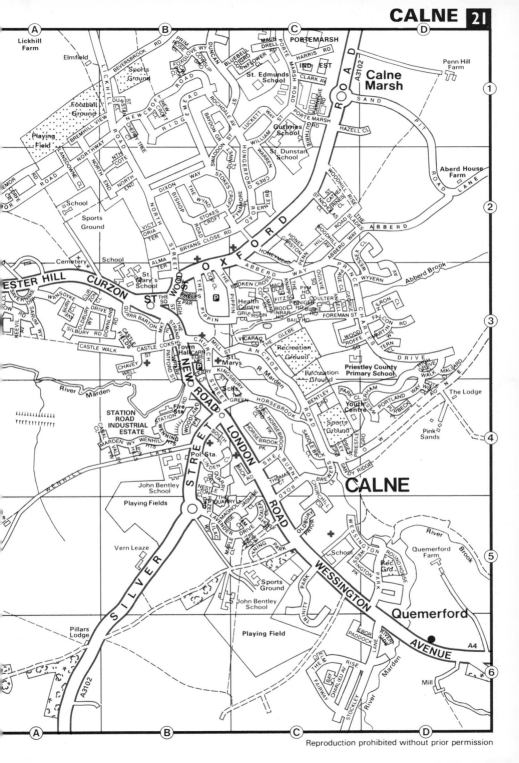

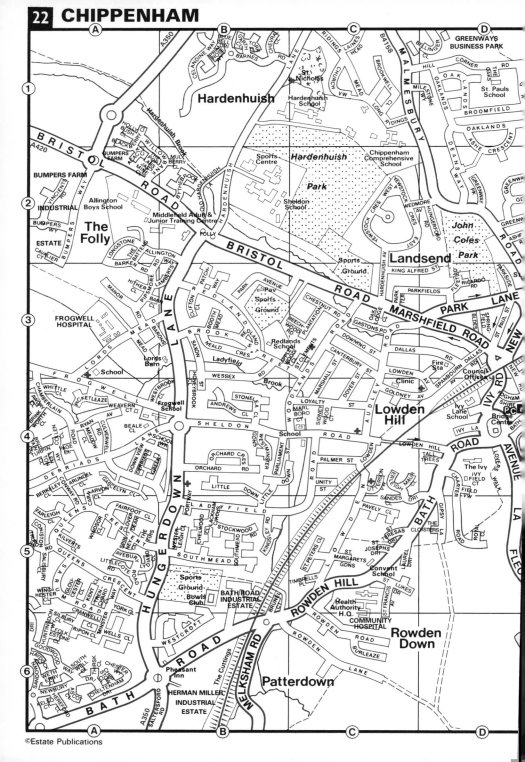

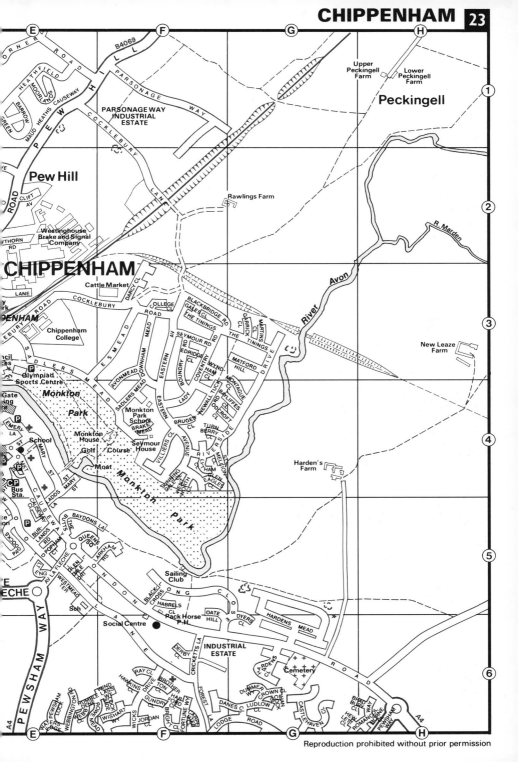

Peckingell

Upper Peckingell Farm
Lower Peckingell Farm

B4069

PARSONAGE WAY INDUSTRIAL ESTATE

PARSONAGE WAY

Pew Hill

Rawlings Farm

R. Marden

Westinghouse Brake and Signal Company

CHIPPENHAM

River Avon

Cattle Market

BLACKBRIDGE RD
GALES CL

COCKLEBURY ROAD

COLLEGE ROAD

THE TININGS

CARRICK CL

MARTINS

New Leaze Farm

Chippenham College

SEYMOUR RD

THE TININGS

EDRIDGE CL

COVENTRY

MATFORD HILL

MONTAGUE

Olympiad Sports Centre

AVONMEAD

SADLERS MEAD

DOWNHAM MEAD

EASTERN AV

BOUNDRY

LADY

WYND HAM

NEWALL TUCK RD

BARCLIFFES CL

RODCROFT

Monkton Park

Monkton Park School

BRAKE MEAD

BRUGES CL

TURN BERRY CL

Harden's Farm

Monkton House

Golf Course

Seymour House

VILLIERS CL

AVENUE

HAM

Moat

Monkton Park

DINNING

NORTH

EAGLES

MELTON

Baydons La
BAYDONS LA

BUR LANDS RD

THE BUTTS

QUEENS SQ

LARKHAM

Sailing Club

LONG CLOSE

Bus Sta.

GLEN DALE

WISSMEAD

BLACKCROSS

HABRELS CL

OATE HILL

DYERS CL

HARDENS MEAD

Social Centre

Rack Horse P.H.

CRICKETTS LA

DERBY CL

INDUSTRIAL ESTATE

Cemetery

PEWSHAM WAY

RAY CL

HAWKINS

BROTHER TON CL

HART CL

FORTUNE WY

FOREST

LODGE ROAD

DANES CL
LUDLOW CL

CROWN CL

CASTLEHAVEN

ROMAN CL

PEWSHAM WAY

A4

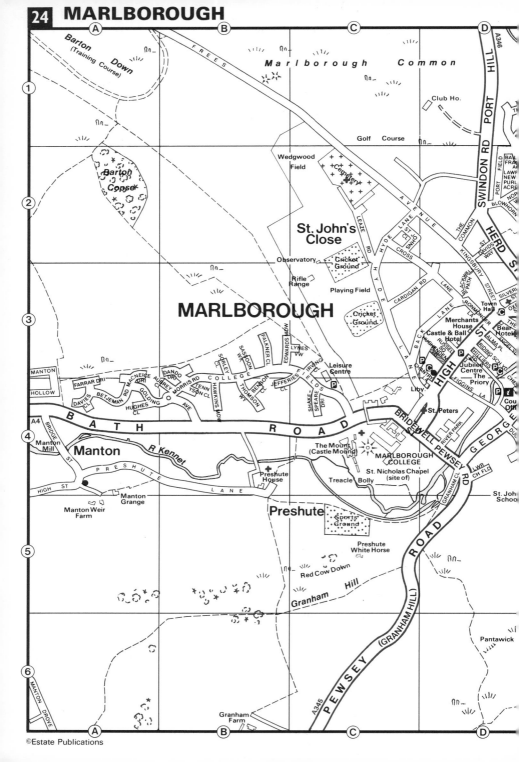

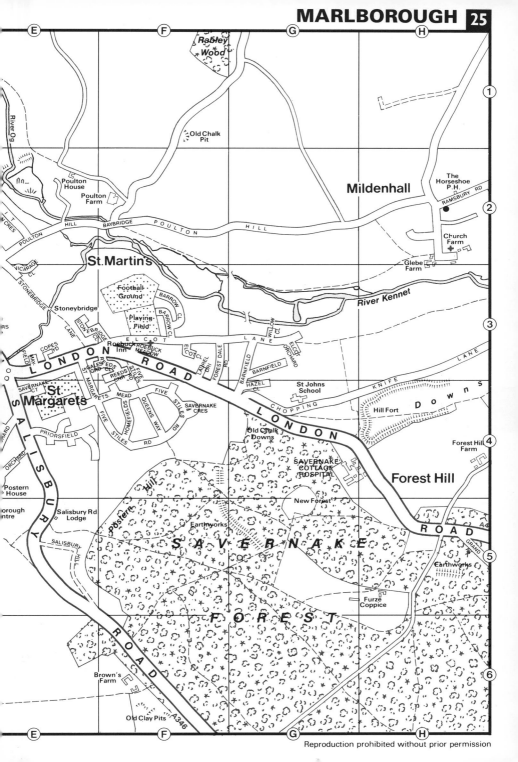

Rabley Wood

E F G H

1

River Og

Old Chalk Pit

The Horseshoe P.H.

Poulton House

Poulton Farm

Mildenhall

RAMSBURY RD

2

HILL BAYBRIDGE POULTON HILL

POULTON

VICARAGE CL

STONEBRIDGE

Church Farm

St. Martins

Glebe Farm

Football Ground

Stoneybridge

BARROW CL

River Kennet

Playing Field

BARROW CL

STONEBRIDGE LANE

ELCOT

3

COPES CYD

Roebuck Inn

ROEBUCK MEADOW

ELCOT CL

LAUREL DRI

FOREST DALE RD

LANE

ELCOT ORCHARD

WILLOW CL

KNIFE LANE

Downs

FIELD WAY

ST. MARGARETS GRD CL

REEDS GRD

SALTED CL

FIVE STILES

BARNFIELD

BARNFIELD

St Johns School

SAVERNAKE CT

St. Margarets

MEAD

QUEENS WAY

FIVE STILES RD

HOMEFIELDS

SAVERNAKE CRES

HAZEL CL

Hill Fort

Forest Hill Farm

4

SALISBURY

PRIORSFIELD

FIVE STILES RD

CHOPPING

LONDON

ROAD

Old Chalk Downs

ORCHARD

Postern House

Salisbury Rd Lodge

SALISBURY

Postern Hill

SAVERNAKE COTTAGE HOSPITAL

Forest Hill

New Forest

ROAD

GRAND

5

Earthworks

SAVERNAKE

Earthworks

Furze Coppice

FOREST

ROAD

6

Brown's Farm

A346

Old Clay Pits

E F G H

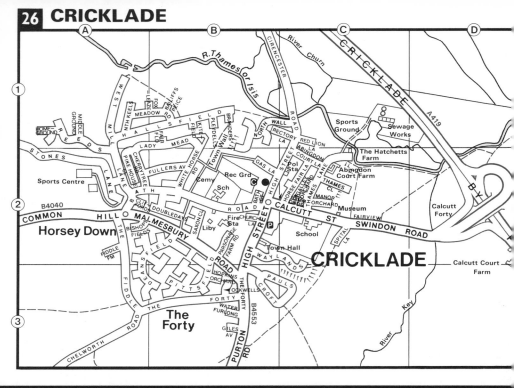

A - Z INDEX TO STREETS
with Postcodes

The Index includes some names for which there is insufficient space on the maps. These names are preceded by an * and are followed by the nearest adjoining thoroughfare.

SWINDON

m Dri North. SN5 14 D3
m Dri South. SN5 14 D4
in Clo. SN3 16 D2
ewood. SN3 17 F4
n Clo. SN5 14 A2
broke Clo. SN4 7 A8
broke Rd. SN2 9 E4
r Clo. SN5 14 A2
e Clo. SN2 8 D2
mbe Rd. SN2 9 E3
m Clo. SN5 14 C3
orth Rd. SN5 14 B2
vell Rd. SN3 16 C1
Copse. SN5 8 B4
dary Clo. SN2 10 C1
e Rd. SN2 9 E4
on Av. SN3 11 E5
rie Av. SN3 16 B4
ymead. SN3 17 F2
ng Grn La. SN1 16 A5
an Clo. SN3 11 E4
od Rd. SN1 15 G4
ll Clo. SN5 8 B6
nham Rd. SN5 14 A3
ord Rd. SN1 3 C6
ey Rd. SN2 10 B3
vell Moor. SN3 17 G5
ar Clo. SN3 16 D5
ole Clo. SN2 10 B5
ole Rd. SN2 10 C5
dean Clo. SN2 9 F1
well Clo. SN2 10 C1
on Clo. SN5 14 B3
some Rd. SN2 9 E3
n Clo. SN2 9 G2
rooke Clo. SN5 8 A6
n Clo. SN3 16 C5
Hill Clo. SN2 9 H2
on Walk. SN3 17 E2
Fields. SN1 16 B1
e End Rd. SN3 10 C6
e St. SN1 3 A2
eman Clo. SN3 11 E4
emead Clo. SN5 14 D1
ewater Clo. SN2 15 F1
ort Rd. SN3 16 D3
Clo. SN3 10 D3
St. SN2 10 B6
Clo. SN3 17 G2
ey Clo. SN2 9 E6
on Rd. SN3 11 E6
St. SN1 15 G2
nia Pl. SN1 3 C6
nia Trade Pk. SN2 10 C4
m Av. SN3 16 C3
St. SN1 3 C2
mead Walk. SN3 17 E1
way. SN2 9 F3
ey Clo. SN3 16 C2
e Clo. SN3 17 F4
Lime Clo. SN2 8 D2
dene. SN2 9 E2
s Clo. SN2 10 B2
sby Way. SN3 11 E6
slands Av. SN2 9 F5
ne Manor La. SN3 16 C5
ning Clo. SN3 11 E3
St. SN2 15 F1
el Gro. SN3 16 B5
Plaza. SN1 3 B3
wick St. SN1 3 B5
ston Way. SN3 17 E2
y Way. SN2 8 D2
urst Cres. SN3 16 D2
ngham Rd. SN3 16 D5
and Clo. SN3 16 D2
ebury Clo. SN3 10 D5
horn Dri. SN2 8 D3
Clo. SN5 8 C4
St. SN2 10 B6
ch Clo. SN3 17 G2
Rd. SN3 10 D5
ge Rd. SN2 9 H1
n Clo. SN3 11 E5
rd Av. SN3 16 B3
ss Clo. SN3 10 D5
ley Clo. SN3 16 D2
t Clo. SN2 8 D2
am Clo. SN3 16 D2
Way. SN2 10 C3
elds. SN5 7 D5
own La. SN2 5 E2
mere. SN3 17 G4
worth St. SN1 15 F2
Rd. SN4 20 C5
d Way. SN3 11 E6
Clo. SN5 14 A3
Ct. SN3 11 G2
St. SN1 3 C4
Dri. SN5 14 A2
y Clo. SN2 10 A4
arvon Wk. SN3 16 C5

Cagney Dri. SN2 9 F1
Cairndown Way. SN2 10 B2
Calder Clo. SN2 9 F2
Calderdale Clo. SN2 5 C4
Callaghan. SN3 10 D4
Callenders. SN5 15 E2
Calvert Rd. SN3 16 B2
Cambria Bri Rd. SN1 15 G2
Cambria Pl. SN1 15 G3
Cambridge Clo. SN3 16 C4
Camden Clo. SN5 14 A3
Cameron Clo. SN3 10 D5
Campden Rd. SN3 16 B3
Campion Gate. SN5 14 A2
Camton Rd. SN5 14 A1
Canal Walk. SN1 3 A3
Canford Clo. SN3 17 E2
Canney Clo. SN4 20 C5
Cannon St. SN1 3 C5
Canterbury Clo. SN3 16 C5
Capesthorne Dri. SN2 9 E1
Capitol Clo. SN3 11 F6
Caprice Clo. SN5 14 A1
Cardigan Clo. SN3 16 C4
Cardwell Clo. SN3 17 E1
Carey Clo. SN5 14 B3
Carfax St. SN1 3 B2
Carisbrook Ter. SN4 20 B5
Carlisle Av. SN3 16 B4
Carlton Gate. SN3 16 D6
Carman Clo. SN3 11 E4
Carpenters La. SN2 10 B6
Carr St. SN1 3 A3
Carraway Dri. SN2 8 C3
Carroll Clo. SN. SN3 17 F4
Carronbridge Rd. SN5 14 C2
Carshalton Rd. SN3 17 E4
Carslake Clo. SN3 17 E3
Carstairs Av. SN3 16 D4
Cartwright Dri. SN5 8 B6
Casson Rd. SN3 10 D4
Castilian Mews. SN5 14 B1
Castle Dore. SN5 14 B3
Castle View Rd. SN4 20 C5
Castlefield Clo. SN5 14 C2
Castleton Rd. SN5 14 A1
Castleview Rd. SN3 11 F5
Catherine St. SN1 3 A3
Catherine Whyte Clo. SN2 9 F3
Catmint Clo. SN2 8 D3
Caulfield Rd. SN2 10 A6
Cavendish Sq. SN3 16 D4
Caversham Clo. SN3 16 C3
Cavie Clo. SN5 8 A6
Caxton Clo. SN3 16 C3
Cayenne Pl. SN2 8 C3
Cecil Rd. SN3 16 D2
Cedars Clo. SN2 9 F4
Centurion Way. SN3 11 F6
Chadworth Gate. SN3 16 C6
Chalford Av. SN3 17 E1
Chamberlain Rd. SN3 10 D4
Chancellor Clo. SN5 14 A2
Chandler Clo. SN1 3 D5
Chandos Clo. SN5 14 B2
Chantry Rd. SN2 9 E4
Chapel Hill. SN2 5 D2
Chapel Rd. SN3 11 G2
Chapel St. SN2 10 B6
Charlbury Clo. SN2 9 E3
Charles McPherson Gdns. SN3 17 F3
Charlfield Clo. SN3 16 D4
Charlotte Mews. SN1 3 D6
Charlton Clo. SN2 10 A2
Charminster Clo. SN3 17 E2
Charolais Dri. SN5 14 B1
Chartley Grn. SN5 14 A3
Chase Wood. SN5 8 A5
Chatsworth Rd. SN2 9 F2
Cheddar Rd. SN2 9 E3
Chelmsford Rd. SN5 14 C1
Cheltenham St. SN1 3 A2
Chelworth Rd. SN2 9 E3
Cheney Manor Ind Est. SN2 9 E5
Cheney Manor Rd. SN2 9 F4
Chepstow Clo. SN5 14 C4
Cheraton Clo. SN3 17 E1
Cherhill Ct. SN2 7 D5
Cherry Brier Clo. SN5 7 E6
Cherry Tree Gro. SN2 9 H4
Chervil Clo. SN2 8 D2
Chesford Clo. SN3 16 D5
Chester St. SN1 3 A3
Chesterfield Clo. SN5 14 C2
Chestnut Av. SN2 10 A4
Chestnut Springs. SN5 7 E6
Chevalier Clo. SN5 14 A1
Cheviot Clo. SN5 14 B2
Chickerell Rd. SN3 16 D2

Chicory Clo. SN2 8 C3
Chilton Clo. SN2 9 E4
Chilworth Clo. SN2 9 E1
Chippenham Clo. SN2 9 G1
Chippenham Way. SN2 9 G1
Chives Way. SN2 8 D3
Chobham Clo. SN3 10 D2
Christie Clo. SN3 17 F4
Chudleigh. SN5 14 B4
Church End. SN5 6 E4
Church Ground. SN3 11 H2
Church Path. SN5 6 D3
Church Pl,. SN5 7 D6
Church Pl. SN1 15 F2
Church Rd. SN1 3 C5
Church St. SN4 20 B5
Church St. SN5 6 D3
Church St. SN3 11 E4
Church Walk. SN2 10 C4
Church Walk Nth. SN2 9 F3
Church Walk Sth. SN2 9 F4
Church Way. SN2 5 D1
Church Way. SN3 10 D5
Churchfield. SN2 9 E2
Churchhill. SN2 5 E2
Churchward Av. SN2 9 F5
Churchward Park. SN5 15 E3
Cirencester Ct. SN1 3 D5
Cirencester Way. SN2 10 B6
Clanfield Rd. SN3 17 E3
Clardon La. SN5 6 D1
Clare Walk. SN5 14 C3
Clarence St. SN1 3 C3
Clarendon La. SN1 15 F3
Clarke Dri. SN5 8 B6
Clary Rd. SN2 8 D2
Clayhill Copse. SN5 8 A5
Clays Clo. SN2 10 B3
Cleasby Clo. SN5 14 D2
Cleeve Lawns. SN3 16 C5
Clevedon Clo. SN3 16 D2
Cleves Clo. SN5 14 B2
Clifton St. SN1 3 A5
Clinton Clo. SN5 14 A3
Cloche Way. SN2 10 C4
Cloudberry Rd. SN2 9 E1
Clouts Wood. SN5 8 B4
Clover Lands. SN2 8 D2
Clover Pk. SN2 8 D3
Clydesdale Clo. SN5 14 B1
Cobden Rd. SN2 9 F6
Colbert Pk. SN2 9 F1
Colbourne St. SN1 3 D1
Colchester Clo. SN5 14 D4
Cole Clo. SN3 17 F2
Colebrook Rd. SN3 11 E6
College Rd. SN5 6 D3
College St. SN1 3 B3
Collett Av. SN2 9 F5
Collingsmead. SN3 17 F3
Collins La. SN5 6 D3
Coln Cres. SN2 9 F2
Colston Clo. SN3 16 D3
Comfrey Clo. SN2 8 D3
Commercial Rd. SN1 3 A3
Commonweal Rd. SN1 15 G4
Compton Clo. SN3 17 E4
Conan Doyle Wk. SN3 17 G4
Conisborough. SN5 14 C3
Conrad Clo. SN3 17 F4
Constable Rd. SN2 10 C4
Constantine Clo. SN3 11 F6
Conway Rd. SN3 17 F4
Conyers Clo. SN5 14 A3
Coombe Rd. SN2 9 E3
Cooper Field. SN2 9 F1
Coppice Clo. SN2 8 D3
Copse Av. SN1 10 C6
Corby Av. SN3 16 B5
Corfe Clo. SN2 9 F3
Corfe Rd. SN5 14 C3
Coriander Way. SN2 8 D2
Corinium Way. SN3 11 F6
Cornflower Rd. SN2 8 D2
Cornmarsh Way. SN3 17 G1
Cornwall Av. SN2 9 G5
Corporation St. SN1 3 B1
Corral Clo. SN5 8 B6
Corsham Rd. SN2 9 H2
Corton Cres. SN5 14 C2
Cotters Clo. SN3 11 E3
Cottington Clo. SN5 14 B4
County Rd. SN1 3 C1
Courtenay Rd. SN3 16 D2
Courtsknap Ct. SN1 15 F3
Covingham Dri. SN3 11 F6
Cowdrey Clo. SN5 14 C4
Cowleaze Walk. SN2 10 C3
Crabtree Copse. SN5 8 B5
Crampton Rd. SN3 16 D1
Cranmore Av. SN3 16 D4
Crawford Clo. SN5 14 B4

Crawley Av. SN3 11 E5
Cricklade Rd. SN2 10 A1
Cricklade St. SN1 3 C5
Crieff Clo. SN3 17 E2
Crispin Clo. SN3 11 E3
Croft Rd. SN1 16 A6
Crombey St. SN1 3 A4
Crompton Rd. SN2 10 A1
Cromwell. SN5 14 B4
Cross St. SN1 3 C4
Crossways Av. SN2 9 H3
Crosswood Rd. SN3 16 D4
Crudwell Way. SN2 9 H1
Cuckoos Mead. SN3 17 G1
Cullerne Rd. SN3 11 F5
Cumberland Rd. SN3 3 D3
Cunetio Rd. SN3 11 F6
Cunningham Rd. SN2 9 G4
Curtis St. SN1 3 A4
Cypress Gro. SN2 9 G4

Dacre Rd. SN3 16 D2
Daisy Clo. SN2 8 D3
Dalefoot Clo. SN5 8 A5
Dallas Av. SN3 17 E1
Dalton Clo. SN3 16 D1
Dalwood Clo. SN3 17 E4
Dammas La. SN1 3 D6
Danestone Clo. SN5 14 A1
Daniel Clo. SN5 15 F3
Darcey Clo. SN5 14 A2
Darius Way. SN2 9 F1
Darnley Clo. SN3 16 C2
Dart Av. SN2 9 G3
Dartmoor Clo. SN5 15 F3
Darwin Clo. SN3 17 E1
Davenham Clo. SN3 16 D4
Davenwood. SN2 10 C2
Davies Pl. SN1 3 A3
Dawlish Rd. SN3 17 E2
Day House La. SN3 17 E5
Days Clo. SN3 10 D5
Deacon St. SN1 3 A4
Dean St. SN1 15 F2
Deben Cres. SN2 9 F2
Deburgh St. SN2 15 F2
Deephurst Way. SN5 14 D3
Delamere Dri. SN3 10 D3
Deloro Ind Est. SN3 10 D4
Delton Business Pk. SN5 14 D2
Denbeck Wood. SN5 14 C1
Denbigh Clo. SN3 16 C4
Denholme. SN3 17 E4
Denholme Rd. SN3 16 D4
Denton Ct. SN3 11 E4
Derby Clo. SN2 9 E5
Derwent Dri. SN2 10 C2
Desborough. SN5 14 B5
Deva Clo. SN3 11 F6
*Devereux Clo, Grindal Dri. SN5 14 A3
Devizes Rd. SN1 3 C6
Devon Rd. SN2 9 G5
Dewberry Clo. SN2 9 E2
Dewell Ms. SN3 3 D6
Dewey Clo. SN4 20 C5
Dexter Clo. SN5 14 B2
Dianmer Clo. SN4 7 A8
Dickens Clo. SN3 17 F4
Dinmore Rd. SN2 9 F1
Dixon St. SN1 3 A4
Dobbin Clo. SN3 17 G1
Dobson Clo. SN2 5 C3
Dockle Way. SN2 10 C3
Dogridge. SN5 6 B3
Don Clo. SN2 9 F2
Donnington Gro. SN3 16 C4
Dorcan Ind Est. SN3 17 G3
Dorcan Way. SN3 17 E1
Dorchester Rd. SN3 16 C4
Dores Ct. SN2 10 B3
Dores Rd. SN3 10 B3
Douglas Rd. SN3 16 C2
Dover St. SN1 3 B4
Dovetrees. SN3 17 G1
Dowling St. SN1 3 B4
Downland Rd. SN2 8 D3
Downs Rd. SN4 20 C5
Downs View. SN5 7 E6
Downs View Rd. SN3 16 B6
Downton Rd. SN2 9 G2
Drakes Way. SN3 16 C2
Draycot Rd. SN4 20 B5
Draycott Clo. SN3 16 D2
Drew St. SN2 15 E1
Drove Rd. SN1 3 D4
Dryden St. SN1 3 A4
Duchess Way. SN2 10 B2
Dudley Rd. SN3 16 C2
Dudmore Rd. SN3 3 D3
Dukes Clo. SN2 10 B2

Dulverton Av. SN3 16 D3
Dunbarton Ter. SN1 3 C4
Dunbeath Rd. SN2 10 B5
Dunraven Clo. SN3 16 C4
Dunsford Clo. SN1 15 F4
Dunster Clo. SN3 16 C5
Dunwich Dri. SN5 14 D3
Durham St. SN1 3 C4
Durnford Rd. SN2 10 A2
Durrington Walk. SN2 9 H2
Dyke Mews. SN4 20 B5

Eagle Clo. SN3 17 G1
Earl Clo. SN5 14 A1
East St. SN1 3 A2
Eastcott Hill. SN1 3 B4
Eastcott Rd. SN1 3 B5
Eastern Av. SN3 16 B2
Eastleaze Rd. SN5 14 C2
Eastmere. SN3 17 G4
Eastville Rd. SN2 9 H3
Eaton Clo. SN3 16 D4
Eaton Wood. SN5 8 B5
Eccleston Clo. SN3 17 E4
Ecklington. SN3 17 E3
Edale Moor. SN3 17 G5
Edgehill. SN5 14 B4
Edgeware Rd. SN1 3 B3
Edgeworth Clo. SN5 14 C1
Edinburgh St. SN2 10 A5
Edington Clo. SN5 14 C3
Edison Rd. SN3 17 F3
Edmund St. SN1 3 B4
Egerton Clo. SN3 17 E1
Elborough Rd. SN2 8 D3
Eldene Dri. SN3 17 E3
Elder Clo. SN2 8 D3
Elgin Dri. SN2 10 B5
Elgin Ind Est. SN2 10 B5
Eliot. SN3 17 G4
Elm Gro. SN5 8 B6
Elm Rd. SN2 9 F4
Elmina Rd. SN1 3 C1
Elmore. SN3 17 F2
Elmswood Clo. SN2 10 B2
Elsham Way. SN2 9 F2
Elsie Hazel Ct. SN5 14 B4
Elstree Way. SN2 9 F1
Ely Clo. SN5 14 D3
Emlyn Sq. SN1 3 A3
Emmanuel Clo. SN2 9 F2
Enford Av. SN2 9 H1
Ensor Clo. SN2 5 C3
Eric Long Clo. SN3 17 F3
Erlestoke Way. SN2 9 H1
Ermin St. SN2 5 C2
Ermin St. SN3 10 C2
Espringham Pl. SN2 10 B2
Essex Walk. SN3 16 C2
Euclid St. SN1 3 C3
Euro Way. SN5 14 A5
Europa Pk Employment Area. SN3 10 D3
Evelyn St. SN3 16 B5
Evergreens Clo. SN3 11 E5
Everleigh Rd. SN2 9 H2
Eworth Clo. SN5 14 A3
Exe Clo. SN2 9 G2
Exeter St. SN1 15 G2
Exmoor Clo. SN2 8 C2
Exmouth St. SN1 15 G3

Fairfax Clo. SN3 16 C1
Fairford Cres. SN2 9 H3
Fairholme Way. SN2 10 C3
Fairlawn. SN3 17 F5
Fairview. SN1 3 A4
Falconscroft. SN3 17 F1
Falmouth Gro. SN3 16 C3
Fanstones Rd. SN3 17 E4
Faraday Rd. SN3 17 G3
Fareham Clo. SN3 17 E3
Faringdon Rd. SN1 3 A3
Farleigh Cres. SN3 16 C5
Farman Clo. SN3 17 F4
Farnborough Rd. SN3 16 D5
Farnsby St. SN1 3 A3
Farrfield. SN2 10 C3
Farriers Clo. SN1 10 B6
Feather Wood. SN5 14 D3
Fenland Clo. SN5 14 A1
Fennel Av. SN2 8 D2
Ferndale Rd. SN2 9 F6
Fernham Rd. SN2 9 E4
Ferrers Dri. SN5 14 A3
Field Rise. SN1 15 G5
Fieldfare. SN3 17 F1
Finchdale. SN3 11 F6
Fir Tree Clo. SN2 9 F4
Firecrest Vw. SN3 17 G2
Firth Clo. SN2 9 F3
Fitzmaurice Clo. SN3 17 F1

29

Southwick Av. SN2 9 G2
Sparcells Dri. SN5 8 C4
Speedwell Clo. SN2 9 E1
Spencer Clo. SN5 14 A1
Spencer Clot. SN3 14 D4
Spersholt. SN5 14 D4
Spring Clo. SN1 3 C3
Spring Gdns. SN1 3 C3
Spring Hill Clo. SN5 14 C3
Springfield Rd. SN1 16 A4
Spur Way. SN2 10 C3
Squires Copse. SN5 8 B5
Stafford St. SN1 14 C3
Stamford Clo. SN5 14 C3
Stanbridge Pk. SN5 14 B1
Stancombe Pk. SN5 14 D3
Standen Way. SN2 5 D4
Standings Clo. SN5 8 A6
Stanier St. SN1 3 B4
Stanley St. SN1 3 C5
Stanmore St. SN1 15 G3
Stansfield Clo. SN5 14 D4
Stanway Clo. SN3 16 D3
Stapleford Clo. SN2 9 G1
Staring Clo. SN5 8 A6
Station App. SN1 3 C6
Station Rd. SN4 20 C5
Station Rd. SN5 6 D2
Station Rd. SN1 3 A2
Stenbury Clo. SN2 5 C4
Stennes Clo. SN5 8 C4
Stephens Rd. SN3 10 D6
Stewart Clo. SN2 9 G1
Stirling Rd. SN3 11 F1
*Stockbridge Copse,
 Ratcombe Rd. SN5 8 B4
Stockton Rd. SN2 9 H2
Stokesay Dri. SN5 14 C3
Stone La. SN5 7 D5
Stonecrop Way. SN2 9 E1
Stonefield Clo. SN5 14 C1
Stonehill Grn. SN5 14 D2
Stonehurst Rd. SN3 10 D6
Stoneybeck Clo. SN5 14 D2
Stratford Clo. SN5 14 D3
Stratton Rd Ind Est.
 SN1 10 C6
Stratton Orchard. SN3 10 D4
Stratton Rd. SN1 10 C6
Stratton St Margaret
 By-Pass. SN2 10 B1
Strouds Hill. SN4 20 B5
Stuart Clo. SN3 16 D2
Stubsmead. SN3 17 F3
Studland Clo. SN3 17 E4
Sudeley Way. SN5 14 B3
Suffolk St. SN2 9 H6
Summers St. SN2 15 F1
Sunningdale Rd. SN2 9 H3
Sunnyside Av. SN1 15 F3
Surrey Rd. SN2 9 F5
Sutton Park. SN2 5 E2
Sutton Rd. SN3 17 F4
Swallowdale. SN3 17 F3
Swallowfield Av. SN3 16 C3
Swanage Walk. SN2 9 E3
Swanbrook. SN3 11 F6
Swindon Rd. SN3 10 D6
Swindon Rd. SN1 3 B5
Swinley Dri. SN5 8 A5
Sword Gdns. SN5 15 F4
Sycamore Gro. SN2 9 H4
Symonds. SN5 14 B5
Syon Clo. SN2 9 F1
Sywell Rd. SN3 11 F6

Tamar Clo. SN2 9 G3
Tamworth Dri. SN5 14 B2
Tansley Moor. SN3 17 G5
Tarragon Clo. SN2 8 C3
Tattershall. SN5 14 C4
Taunton St. SN1 15 G2
Tavistock Rd. SN3 17 E2
Tawny Owl Clo. SN3 11 E6
Taylor Cres. SN3 10 D2
Tealsbrook. SN3 17 G1
Techno Trading Est.
 SN2 10 C5
Tedder Clo. SN2 9 G5
Tees Clo. SN2 9 F2
Teeswater Clo. SN5 14 B2
Telford Way. SN5 14 B2
Temple St. SN1 3 B3
Tenby. SN3 16 C4
Tennyson St. SN1 3 A3
Tensing Gdns. SN2 9 H3
Terncliff. SN3 17 F1
Tewkesbury Way. SN5 14 A1
Thackeray Clo. SN3 17 F4
Thames Av. SN2 9 E2
Thamesdown Dri,
 Abbey Meads. SN2 5 C4

Thamesdown Dri,
 Haydon. SN2 8 C3
The Acorns. SN3 16 D5
The Beeches. SN5 7 C5
The Birches. SN3 16 D5
The Bramptons. SN5 14 C1
The Brow. SN2 9 E2
The Bungalows. SN2 9 G4
The Buntings. SN3 17 F1
The Butts. SN5 7 D6
The Canney. SN4 20 C5
The Chesters. SN5 14 D2
The Circle. SN5 7 D6
The Close. SN5 7 D6
The Close. SN3 11 E4
The Common. SN5 6 C2
The Copse. SN5 5 D2
The Crescent. SN5 8 A4
The Crescent. SN4 20 B6
The Curnicks. SN4 20 95
The Drive. SN3 17 E1
The Ferns. SN2 9 H6
The Forum. SN3 14 C3
The Fox. SN5 6 F4
The Harriers. SN3 17 F1
The Heights. SN1 15 F4
The Holbein. SN5 14 B3
The Hyde. SN5 6 D3
The Knoll. SN2 16 A5
The Mall. SN1 3 A5
The Masons. SN5 6 B3
The Mews. SN5 7 E6
The Orchard. SN4 20 C5
The Orchards. SN3 16 C6
The Owletts. SN3 17 G1
The Paddocks. SN3 10 D5
The Paddocks. SN5 7 E6
The Parade. SN1 3 B3
The Peak. SN5 6 C3
The Planks. SN3 3 D6
The Quarries. SN1 15 H4
The Ridge. SN2 5 D2
The Ridgeway. SN4 20 C6
The Square. SN1 3 D6
The Street. SN5 7 D6
The Street. SN3 9 E3
The Weavers. SN3 3 D6
Theatre Sq. SN1 3 B3
Theobald St. SN1 15 G2
Thirlmere. SN3 17 G4
Thomas St. SN2 15 F1
Thornbridge Av. SN3 16 D4
Thorne Rd. SN3 17 F4
Thornford Dri. SN3 14 C2
Thornhill Dri. SN2 5 B3
Thornhill Ind Est. SN3 11 G3
Thornhill Rd. SN3 11 G4
Thrushel Clo. SN2 9 E3
Thurleston Rd. SN3 16 B3
Thurney Dri. SN5 14 A3
Thyme Clo. SN2 8 C3
Tidworth Clo. SN5 15 E4
Tilleys La. SN3 10 D5
Tilshead Walk. SN2 9 H1
Timandra Clo. SN2 9 F1
Tintagel Clo. SN5 14 C4
Tisbury Clo. SN2 9 H1
Tismeads Cres. SN1 16 A5
Titchfield Clo. SN5 14 A3
Tithe Barn Cres. SN1 15 F4
Tiverton Rd. SN2 9 H5
Tockenham Way. SN2 9 G1
Tollard Way. SN3 17 F2
Torridge Clo. SN2 9 E3
Totterdown Clo. SN3 17 G1
Tovey Rd. SN2 9 G5
Towcester Rd. SN3 11 E6
Tower Rd. SN5 8 B5
Tracy Clo. SN2 9 F1
Trajan Rd. SN3 11 F6
Transfer Bridge Ind Est.
 SN1 10 B6
Tree Courts Rd. SN2 9 G1
Tregantle Walk. SN3 17 E2
Tregoze Way. SN5 14 A2
Trent Rd. SN2 9 F3
Trentham Clo. SN3 16 D4
Trinity Clo. SN3 16 D4
Trueman Clo. SN3 17 F3
Truro Path. SN5 14 C3
Tryon Clo. SN3 17 G5
Tudor Cres. SN3 11 E5
Tulip Tree Clo. SN2 9 H4
Turl St. SN1 3 B2
Turnball. SN4 20 B5
Turner St. SN1 15 F3
Turnham Grn. SN5 14 B4
Turnpike Rd. SN6 5 D3
Tweed Clo. SN2 9 E2
Twyford Clo. SN3 16 D1
Tyburn Clo. SN5 14 B2
Tydeman St. SN2 10 A5

Tye Gdns. SN5 14 A3
Tyndale Path. SN5 14 A2
Tyneham Rd. SN3 17 E2

Ullswater Clo. SN3 17 G4
Union Row. SN1 3 C5
Union St. SN1 3 C5
Upfield. SN3 17 G4
Upham Rd. SN3 17 F1
Upper Pavenhill. SN5 6 A3
Utah Clo. SN5 15 E4
Uxbridge Rd. SN5 14 A4

Valleyside. SN1 15 F4
Vanburgh Gate. SN3 16 D6
Vasterne Clo. SN5 6 C2
Ventnor Clo. SN2 9 E3
Verney Clo. SN3 17 G2
Verulam Clo. SN3 11 F6
Verwood Clo. SN3 16 D3
Vespasian Clo. SN3 11 F6
Vicarage Rd. SN2 9 F5
Victoria Rd. SN2 3 C4
Vilett St. SN1 3 A3
Villiers Clo. SN5 14 A2
Viscount Way. SN3 11 F1
Volpe Clo. SN5 14 A3
Volta Rd. SN1 3 C2

Wagtail Clo. SN3 11 E6
Wainwright Clo. SN3 17 F3
Waite Meads Clo. SN5 6 D2
Wakefield Clo. SN5 8 B3
Walcot Rd. SN3 3 D4
Wallingford Clo. SN5 14 C3
Wallis Dri. SN2 5 C3
Wallsworth Rd. SN3 16 D3
Walnut Tree Gdns. SN5 7 E6
Walsingham Rd. SN3 16 C2
Walter Clo. SN5 14 B2
Walton Clo. SN3 16 D3
Walwayne Field. SN3 10 D2
Wanborough Rd,
 Covingham. SN3 17 G1
Wanborough Rd,
 Lower Stratton. SN3 11 F5
Warbeck Gate. SN5 14 B4
Wardley Clo. SN3 16 D4
Wardour Clo. SN3 16 C5
Wareham Clo. SN5 14 B5
Warminster Av. SN3 9 H1
Warneford Clo. SN5 14 D4
Warner Clo. SN3 11 E3
Warwick Rd. SN1 3 B4
Water Field. SN5 6 B3
Watercrook Mews. SN5 14 D3
Waterdown Rd. SN3 8 C2
Watermead. SN3 11 F4
Watling Clo. SN2 15 E2
Wavell Rd. SN2 9 G4
Waverley Rd. SN3 11 E6
Wayside Clo. SN3 15 E1
Webbs Wood. SN5 8 B4
Wedgewood Clo. SN2 15 F1
Weedon Rd. SN3 11 E6
Welcombe Av. SN3 16 D3
Welford Clo. SN3 11 E6
Well Clo. SN4 20 B5
Wellington St. SN1 3 B2
Wells St. SN1 3 C3
Welton Rd. SN5 14 D2
Wembley St. SN3 14 D2
Wensleydale Clo. SN5 14 B2
Wentworth Park. SN5 14 B3
Wesley St. SN1 3 C5
West End Rd. SN3 10 D5
West Hill. SN2 5 D1
West Mead. SN5 14 D1
Westbrook Rd. SN2 9 G5
Westbury Rd. SN3 9 H2
Westcott Pl. SN1 15 F3
Westcott St. SN1 15 F3
Western St. SN1 3 C4
Westfield Way. SN3 8 D3
Westlea. SN5 14 C2
Westlecot Rd. SN1 15 G5
Westmead Ind Est. SN3 14 D1
Westminster Rd. SN5 14 D1
Westmorland Rd. SN1 3 D4
Westview Walk. SN3 17 E1
Westwood Rd. SN2 9 H1
Wey Clo. SN3 9 G2
Weyhill Clo. SN3 16 D3
Wheatlands. SN3 9 E3
Wheatstone Rd. SN3 17 G3
Wheeler Av. SN2 10 B4
Whilestone Way. SN3 11 E5
Whitbourne Av. SN3 16 C3
Whitbred Clo. SN5 14 B1
Whitby Gro. SN3 9 F6
White Castle. SN5 14 C4
White Edge Moor. SN3 17 G5

Whitefield Cres. SN5 8 A5
Whitehead St. SN1 3 A4
Whitehill Way. SN5 14 A4
Whitehouse Rd. SN2 9 H6
Whitelands Rd. SN3 10 D6
Whiteman St. SN2 9 H6
Whitgift Clo. SN5 14 A2
Whitmore Clo. SN5 14 A2
Whitney St. SN1 3 B4
Whittington Rd. SN5 14 C2
Whitworth Rd. SN2 9 H6
Wichelstok Clo. SN1 15 H5
Wick La. SN3 17 G6
Wickdown Av. SN2 9 E4
Wicks Clo. SN2 9 E2
Widham. SN5 6 D2
Widhill La. SN2 5 C2
Wigmore Av. SN3 16 C4
Wilcot Av. SN2 10 A2
Wilcox Clo. SN2 9 H4
Wildern Sq. SN3 17 E2
Wilkins Clo. SN2 10 C2
William St. SN1 15 G3
Willis Way. SN5 6 C3
Willowbrook. SN5 6 D3
Willowherb Clo. SN2 9 E1
Willows Av. SN2 10 A3
Wills Av. SN1 10 C6
Wilmot Clo. SN5 14 A2
Wilson Rd. SN3 17 F3
Wilton Walk. SN2 9 H1
Wiltshire Av. SN2 9 G6
Wimpole Clo. SN3 16 D4
Winchcombe Clo. SN5 14 A2
Winchester Clo. SN3 11 E5
Windbrook Mdw. SN3 10 D3
Windermere. SN3 17 G4
Windflower Rd. SN2 9 E1
Windmill Hill Business Pk.
 SN5 14 A4
Windmill Piece. SN4 20 C5
Windrush Rd. SN2 9 F3
Windsor Clo. SN2 9 H2
Windsor Rd. SN4 7 A8
Wingfield. SN3 10 D2
Wingfield Av. SN2 9 E4
Winifred St. SN3 16 B4
Winlaw Clo. SN5 14 C1
Winsley Clo. SN2 9 H2
Winstanley Clo. SN5 14 B4
Winterslow Rd. SN2 9 G2
Winwick Rd. SN5 14 B4
Wiseman Clo. SN2 17 G2
Witfield Clo. SN5 6 C2
Witham Way. SN3 10 C2
Witts La. SN5 6 C2
Woburn Clo. SN3 9 F1
Wolsely Av. SN3 16 D4
Wood Hall Dri. SN2 8 D3
Wood St. SN1 16 A4
Woodbine Ter. SN3 17 F5
Woodbury Clo. SN5 8 A6
Woodchesters. SN5 14 C2
Woodside Av. SN3 16 C3
*Woodspring Ct,
 Grovelands Av. SN1 15 H5
Woodstock Rd. SN3 11 E6
Woollaton Clo. SN5 14 B3
Wootton Bassett Rd.
 SN1 15 E3
Wordsworth Dri. SN2 10 C2
Worlidge Dri. SN5 14 C1
Worsley Rd. SN5 14 A4
Wrenswood. SN3 17 F1
Wylye Clo. SN2 9 E3
Wynndale Cres. SN3 10 D2
Wyvern Clo. SN1 16 A5

Yardley Clo. SN3 9 E4
Yarmouth Clo. SN3 14 B3
Yarnton Clo. SN5 8 B6
Yarrow Clo. SN2 8 D3
Yeats Clo. SN2 5 C3
*Yellowhammer Clo,
 Wagtail Clo. SN3 11 E6
Yeoman Clo. SN5 14 A1
Yeovil Clo. SN3 17 E3
Yew Tree Gdns. SN3 11 G3
Yiewsley Cres. SN3 11 E5
York Rd. SN1 3 C4

CALNE

Abberd La. SN11 21 D2
Abberd Way. SN11 21 C3
Alma Ter. SN11 21 B2
Anchor Rd. SN11 21 C3
Angell Clo. SN11 21 C3
Avebury Clo. SN11 21 A3

Azalea Clo. SN11
Back Rd. SN11
Baily Ho. SN11
Bay Clo. SN11
Baydon Gro. SN11
Bentley Gro. SN11
Beversbrook Rd. SN11
Bishop Rd. SN11
Blake Ho. SN11
Bluebell Gro. SN11
Bodinnar Ho. SN11
Braemor Rd. SN11
Bremhill Vw. SN11
Brewers La. SN11
Broken Cross. SN11
Bryans Close Rd. SN11
Campion Clo. SN11
Canal Clo. SN11
Carnegie Mews. SN11
Carnegie Rd. SN11
Carpenters Clo. SN11
Castle St. SN11
Castle Walk. SN11
Castlefields. SN11
Charlieu Av. SN11
Chavey Well Ct. SN11
Cherry Tree Ct. SN11
Chilvester Hill. SN11
Church St. SN11
Churchill Clo. SN11
Clark Av. SN11
Colemans Clo. SN11
Cop Croft. SN11
Corfe Cres. SN11
Cornflower Clo. SN11
Cotswold Clo. SN11
Coulter Ho. SN11
Cowslip Gro. SN11
Coxs Hill. SN11
Curzon Clo. SN11
Curzon St. SN11
Dixon Way. SN11
Downland Rd. SN11
Druids Clo. SN11
Duncan St. SN11
Dunnet Clo. SN11
Ebor Paddock. SN11
Elm Clo. SN11
Ernle Rd. SN11
Fairway. SN11
Falcon Rd. SN11
Fitzmaurice Sq. SN11
Foreman St. SN11
Foxglove Way. SN11
Fynamore Pl. SN11
George Clo. SN11
Grierson Clo. SN11
Guthrie Clo. SN11
Harris Rd. SN11
Hazel Gro. SN11
Hazell Clo. SN11
Heather Way. SN11
Heron Clo. SN11
High St. SN11
Highgrove Clo. SN11
Holly Clo. SN11
Honey Garston. SN11
Honeymead. SN11
Horsebrook. SN11
Horsebrook Pk. SN11
Hungerford Rd. SN11
INDUSTRIAL ESTATES:
Portemarsh Ind Est.
 SN11
Station Rd Ind Est.
 SN11
Jasmine Clo. SN11
Keevil Av. SN11
Kerry Cres. SN11
Kingsbury St. SN11
Lansdowne Clo. SN11
Lickhill Rd. SN11
Lilac Way. SN11
Lime Tree Clo. SN11
Linden Clo. SN11
*Lodge Clo, Longbarrow
 SN11
London Rd. SN11
Longbarrow Rd. SN11
Low La. SN11
Luckett Way. SN11
Macaulay Sq. SN11
Magnolia Rise. SN11
Mallard Clo. SN11
Maple Clo. SN11
Marden Way. SN11
Market Hill. SN11
Martin Way. SN11
Maundrell Rd. SN11
Mill St. SN11
Nesleton Clo. SN11
New Rd. SN11

...roft Clo. SN11 21 B1
...roft Rd. SN11 21 B1
...End. SN11 21 A2
...St. SN11 21 B2
...cote. SN11 21 B2
...way. SN11 21 A2
...le Sq. SN11 21 C3
...ury Prior. SN11 21 C5
...ury Way. SN11 21 A3
...ard Clo. SN11 21 C4
...rd Rd. SN11 21 B3
...Clo. SN11 21 C3
...rd St. SN11 21 C4
...Hill Rd. SN11 21 B3
...s Par. SN11 21 C2
...ls. SN11 21 B3
...ger Ho. SN11 21 B4
...Marsh Rd. SN11 21 C1
...and Way. SN11 21 D4
...ley Gro. SN11 21 D4
...ose Clo. SN11 21 B1
...e Charles Dri.
...11 21 C3
...eck Clo. SN11 21 D4
...eck Pl. SN11 21 D4
...Ho. SN11 21 C3
...Barton. SN11 21 B3
...rydale Clo. SN11 21 B4
...mead. SN11 21 B1
...side. SN11 21 D6
...dale Av. SN11 21 B1
...dhouse. SN11 21 D5
...le Back Clo. SN11 21 C4
...therines Clo. SN11 21 C2
...nstan Clo. SN11 21 B1
...cholas Clo. SN11 21 C2
...Pit Rd. SN11 21 D1
...y Ridge. SN11 21 C4
...n Way. SN11 21 A3
...rnake Dri. SN11 21 A3
...ourne Rd. SN11 21 C4
...ury Rd. SN11 21 A3
...r St. SN11 21 B5
...n Pl. SN11 21 B4
...on Rd. SN11 21 B4
...ley La. SN11 21 C6
...es Croft. SN11 21 B2
...ldon St. SN11 21 B2
...arisk Clo. SN11 21 C5
...Clo. SN11 21 D3
...Glebe. SN11 21 C3
...Green. SN11 21 C4
...Knapp. SN11 21 B3
...Pippin. SN11 21 B5
...Quarry. SN11 21 B5
...Rise. SN11 21 C2
...Slades. SN11 21 C2
...Square. SN11 21 B3
...Strand. SN11 21 B3
...Wharf. SN11 21 B3
...Wynd. SN11 21 B2
...nas Ct. SN11 21 C4
...y Pk. SN11 21 C5
...g Pk. SN11 21 C5
...y View. SN11 21 B4
...age Clo. SN11 21 C3
...ria Ter. SN11 21 B2
...ter Sutton Clo,
...ngbarrow Rd. SN11 21 A3
...sdyke Dri. SN11 21 A3
...en Cres. SN11 21 C2
...hill Heights. SN11 21 B4
...hill La. SN11 21 A4
...sex Clo. SN11 21 D3
...sington Av. SN11 21 C5
...sington Pk. SN11 21 D5
...erhan Wk. SN11 21 D4
...am St. SN11 21 C1
...d St. SN11 21 B3
...dhill Av. SN11 21 C2
...dhill Rise. SN11 21 C2
...dland Pk. SN11 21 B4
...droffe Sq. SN11 21 C3
...ern Av. SN11 21 D3
...Tree Clo. SN11 21 A3

CHIPPENHAM

...ia Clo. SN14 22 A2
...gton Way. SN14 22 A2
...ews Clo. SN14 22 B4
...ewood Clo. SN14 22 C3
...del Clo. SN14 22 A4
...t Clo. SN14 22 B4
...Cres. SN15 22 D1
...ield Rd. SN14 22 D2
...ey Rd. SN14 22 C4
...ury Rd. SN14 22 A5

Avenue La Fleche. SN15 22 D4
Avonmead. SN15 23 F3
Awdry Clo. SN14 22 A2
Barken Rd. SN14 22 A2
Barn Clo. SN14 22 A3
Barnes Rd. SN14 22 B1
Barons Mead. SN14 22 A3
Barrow Grn. SN15 23 E1
Bath Rd. SN14 22 A6
Bath Rd. SN15 22 C5
Baydons La. SN15 23 E5
Bayliffes Clo. SN15 23 G4
Beale Clo. SN14 22 A4
Beaver Mead. SN15 23 F6
Beechwood Rd. SN14 22 C3
Bellinger Clo. SN15 22 D1
Berkeley Clo. SN14 22 A4
Birch Gro. SN15 22 D2
Birds Marsh View. SN15 23 E1
Blackberry Clo. SN14 22 A1
Blackbridge Rd. SN15 23 F3
Blackcross. SN15 23 F5
Bluebell Dri. SN14 22 B1
Boothmead. SN14 22 B3
Borough Par. SN15 22 D4
Boundry Rd. SN15 23 F3
Bradbury Clo. SN15 23 G6
Brake Mead. SN15 23 F4
Bright Clo. SN15 23 F6
Brinkworth Clo. SN14 22 A4
Bristol Rd. SN15 22 A1
Brittain Clo. SN14 22 A4
Brook St. SN14 22 B3
Brookwell Clo. SN15 22 C1
Broomfield. SN15 22 D1
Brotherton Clo. SN15 23 F6
Bruges Clo. SN15 23 F4
Brunel Ct. SN15 22 B5
Bulls Hill. SN15 23 E5
Bumpers Way. SN14 22 A2
Burlands Rd. SN15 23 E5
Burleaze. SN15 22 C6
Bythebrook. SN14 22 B2
Canterbury St. SN14 22 C3
Carnarvon Clo. SN14 22 A5
Carpenter Clo. SN15 23 F6
Castlehaven Clo. SN15 23 G6
Causeway. SN15 23 E4
Causeway Clo. SN15 23 E5
Cavalier Ct. SN14 22 A2
Cedar Gro. SN15 23 E2
Celandine Way. SN14 22 B1
Chamberlain Rd. SN14 22 A4
Chapel La. SN15 23 E4
Charter Rd. SN15 22 D4
Cheltenham Dri. SN14 22 A6
Chelwood Clo. SN14 22 B5
Chepstow Clo. SN14 22 A6
Chester Way. SN14 22 A6
Chestnut Rd. SN14 22 C3
Chevral Clo. SN15 22 B1
Church View. SN15 22 C1
Clift Av. SN15 23 E2
Clift Ho. SN15 22 D2
Clifton Clo. SN14 22 B3
Clover Dean. SN14 22 A5
Cocklebury La. SN15 23 E1
Cocklebury Rd. SN15 23 E3
Colborne Clo. SN15 23 H6
College Clo. SN15 23 F3
Collen Clo. SN14 22 A4
Coniston Rd. SN14 22 A5
Conway Rd. SN14 22 A4
Cranwell Clo. SN14 22 A6
Cricketts La. SN15 23 F6
Crown Clo. SN15 23 G6
Culverwell Rd. SN14 22 A4
Dallas Rd. SN15 22 C3
Danes Clo. SN15 23 F6
Darcy Clo. SN15 23 F3
Deansway. SN15 22 D1
Derby Clo. SN15 23 F6
Derriads Grn. SN14 22 A4
Derriads La. SN14 22 A4
Dover St. SN15 22 D3
Down View. SN14 22 B4
Downham Mead. SN15 23 F3
Downing St. SN14 22 C3
Dummer Way. SN15 23 G6
Dyers Clo. SN15 23 G6
Eastern Av. SN15 23 F3
Edridge Clo. SN15 23 F3
Elmwood. SN15 23 E1
Emery La. SN15 23 E4
Erleigh Dri. SN15 22 C4
Esmead. SN15 23 F3
Fairfoot Clo. SN14 22 A5
Farleigh Clo. SN14 22 A5
Field Vw. SN15 22 D4
Fleet Rd. SN15 22 D3

Foghamshire. SN15 22 D4
Folkestone Clo. SN14 22 A6
Forest La. SN15 23 F6
Fortune Way. SN15 23 F6
Foundry La. SN15 23 E3
Frogwell. SN14 22 A3
Gales Clo. SN15 23 F3
Garrick Clo. SN15 23 G3
Garth Clo. SN14 22 B1
Gascelyn Clo. SN14 22 A4
Gastons Rd. SN14 22 C3
Gipsy La. SN15 22 D5
Gladstone Rd. SN15 22 D4
Glendale Dri. SN15 23 E5
Gleneagles Clo. SN15 23 F4
Gloucester Clo. SN14 22 A5
Goldney Av. SN15 22 C4
Goodwood Way. SN14 22 A6
Greenway Av. SN15 22 D2
Greenway Ct. SN15 22 D1
Greenway Gdns. SN15 22 D2
Greenway La. SN15 22 D1
Greenway Pk. SN15 22 D2
Gundry Clo. SN15 23 F6
Habrels Clo. SN15 23 F5
Hancock Clo. SN15 23 G6
Hardenhuish Av. SN15 22 C3
Hardenhuish La. SN15 22 B2
Hardens Clo. SN15 23 G6
Hardens Mead. SN15 23 G6
Harford Clo. SN15 23 F6
Hawkins Clo. SN15 23 F6
Hawthorn Rd. SN15 23 E2
Haydock Clo. SN14 22 A6
Heathfield. SN15 23 E1
Hereford Clo. SN14 22 A6
Hewlett Clo. SN15 23 G6
High St. SN15 23 E4
Hill Corner Rd. SN15 22 D1
Hill Rise. SN15 22 D1
Hither Clo. SN14 22 A3
Hollybush Clo. SN14 22 A1
Honeybrook Clo. SN14 22 B3
Hungerdown La. SN14 22 A2
Hungerford Rd. SN15 22 D2
Huntingdon Way. SN14 22 A6
INDUSTRIAL ESTATES:
Bath Rd Ind Est. SN14 22 B5
Bumpers Farm Ind Est. SN14 22 A2
Greenways Business Park. SN15 22 D1
Herman Miller Ind Est. SN14 22 B6
Parsonage Way Ind Est. SN15 23 F1
Ivy Field Ct. SN15 22 D4
Ivy La. SN15 22 D4
Ivy Rd. SN15 22 D4
Jasmine Clo. SN14 22 A2
Jordan Clo. SN15 23 F6
Kelso Ct. SN14 22 A6
Kent Clo. SN14 22 A5
Kilverts Clo. SN14 22 A5
King Alfred St. SN15 22 C3
Kingsley Rd. SN14 22 B5
Lackham Circus. SN14 22 B5
Ladds La. SN15 23 E5
Lady Coventry Rd. SN15 23 F4
Ladyfield Rd. SN14 22 B5
Laines Head. SN15 22 C1
Lamberts. SN14 22 B3
Langley Rd. SN15 23 E2
Lansdown Gro. SN15 23 E2
Larkham Rise. SN15 23 F5
Laurel Rd. SN14 22 C5
Lenton Clo. SN14 22 A4
Little Down. SN14 22 B4
Little Englands. SN15 23 E5
Littlecote Rd. SN14 22 A5
Lockside. SN15 23 F6
Lodge Rd. SN15 23 G6
London Rd. SN15 23 F5
Long Clo. SN15 23 F5
Long Ridings. SN15 22 C1
Longstone. SN14 22 A2
Lords Mead. SN14 22 A3
Lovers Walk. SN15 22 D4
Lowden. SN14 22 C5
Lowden Av. SN15 22 C3
Lowden Hill. SN15 22 C4
Loyalty St. SN14 22 C4
Ludlow Clo. SN15 23 G6
Lydiard Clo. SN15 22 A5
Lytham Clo. SN14 23 F4
Malmesbury Rd. SN15 22 C1
Manor Rd. SN14 22 A3
Maple Way. SN15 22 D1
Market Pl. SN15 23 E4
Marlborough Ct. SN14 22 C4
Marshall St. SN15 22 C4

Marshfield Rd. SN15 22 C3
Martins Clo. SN15 23 G3
Matford Hill. SN15 23 G3
Maud Heaths Causeway. SN15 23 E1
Maur Clo. SN15 22 C4
Meadow Clo. SN14 22 A4
Melksham Rd. SN15 22 B6
Milestone Way. SN15 22 D1
Minster Way. SN14 22 A6
Monkton Hill. SN15 22 D3
Montague Clo. SN15 23 G4
Moorlands. SN15 23 E1
Mulberry Clo. SN14 22 B2
Murrayfield. SN15 23 E2
Neald Cres. SN14 22 B3
New La. SN15 22 D3
New Rd. SN15 22 D3
Newall Tuck Rd. SN15 23 F4
Newbury Rd. SN14 22 A6
Northwood. SN15 23 E1
Oak Lodge Clo. SN15 22 C3
Oaklands. SN15 22 D1
Oate Hill. SN15 23 F5
Odcroft Clo. SN15 23 F4
Old Hardenhuish La. SN14 22 B2
Old Rd. SN15 22 D3
Orchard Cres. SN14 22 B4
Orchard Rd. SN14 22 B4
Page Clo. SN15 23 F6
Palmer St. SN14 22 C4
Park Av. SN14 22 B3
Park La. SN15 22 D3
Park Ter. SN15 22 C3
Parkfields. SN15 22 C3
Parkside. SN15 22 D3
Parliament St. SN14 22 B4
Parsonage Way. SN15 23 F1
Patchway. SN14 22 B3
Pavely Clo. SN15 22 C5
Pew Hill. SN15 23 E1
Pewsham Lock. SN15 23 E6
Pewsham Way. SN15 23 E6
Picketleaze. SN14 22 A4
Pipsmore Rd. SN14 22 A3
Plantation. SN14 22 C3
Popham Ct. SN15 23 E5
Portway. SN14 22 B5
Primrose Way. SN14 22 B1
Queens Cres. SN14 22 A5
Queens Sq. SN15 23 E5
Ray Clo. SN15 23 F6
Redland. SN14 22 B3
Ricardo Rd. SN15 22 D3
Ridings Mead. SN15 22 C1
Ripon Clo. SN14 22 A6
Riverside Dri. SN15 23 F4
Roman Way. SN15 23 G6
Rowden Hill. SN15 22 C6
Rowden La. SN15 22 C6
Rowden Rd. SN15 22 C6
Rowe Mead. SN15 23 E6
Royal Clo. SN15 22 D5
Rumble Dene. SN15 23 E6
Ryan Av. SN14 22 A4
Sadlers Mead. SN15 23 E3
St Clements Ct. SN14 22 C3
St Francis Clo. SN15 22 C5
St Josephs Dri. SN15 22 C5
St Lukes Dri. SN15 22 C5
St Margarets Gdns. SN15 23 C5
St Mary St. SN15 23 E4
St Marys Pl. SN15 22 D3
St Mellion Clo. SN15 23 F4
St Paul St. SN15 22 D3
St Peters Clo. SN15 22 C5
St Teresa's Dri. SN15 22 C5
Salisbury Clo. SN15 22 A5
Saltersford Rd. SN14 22 A6
Sandes Clo. SN15 22 C4
Sandown Dri. SN14 22 A5
Sarum Rd. SN14 22 A5
Saxon St. SN14 22 B3
School Walk. SN14 22 A4
Seymour St. SN15 23 F3
Sheldon Rd. SN14 22 B4
Sidney Wood Ct. SN14 22 C4
Silbury Clo. SN14 22 A6
Southmead. SN14 22 B5
Southwell Clo. SN14 22 A6
Spanbourn Av. SN15 22 D4
Spinney Clo. SN14 22 A4
Springfields Blds. SN15 22 D3
Station Hill. SN15 22 D3
Stockwood Rd. SN14 22 B5
Stonelea Clo. SN14 22 B4
Sunningdale Clo. SN15 23 F4
Tall Trees. SN15 22 D4
The Battens. SN15 22 A2
The Bridge. SN15 22 D4

The Butts. SN14 23 E5
The Cloisters. SN15 22 D5
The Firs. SN14 22 A5
The Hamlet. SN15 22 D2
The Oaks. SN15 22 D1
The Paddocks. SN15 23 E5
The Poplars. SN14 22 A2
The Tinings. SN15 23 F3
Thirsk Clo. SN14 22 A6
Timber St. SN15 23 E4
Timbrells Pl. SN15 22 C5
Torr Clo. SN14 22 B1
Truro Walk. SN14 22 A5
Tugela Rd. SN15 23 E2
Turnberry Clo. SN15 23 F4
Turpin Way. SN14 22 A4
Twickenham Way. SN15 23 E2
Union St. SN15 22 D3
Unity St. SN14 22 C4
Utterson View. SN15 22 C4
Villiers Clo. SN15 23 F4
Vincients Rd. SN14 22 A2
Waters Edge. SN15 23 E6
Weavern Ct. SN14 23 E6
Webb Clo. SN15 23 E6
Webbington Rd. SN15 23 E6
Wedmore Av. SN15 22 C2
Wells Clo. SN14 22 A6
Wentworth Clo. SN14 23 F4
Wessex Rd. SN14 22 B3
Westbrook Clo. SN14 22 A4
Westcroft. SN14 22 B6
Westerleigh Clo. SN14 22 B5
Westmead La. SN15 22 D5
Westmead Ter. SN15 23 E5
Westminster Gdns. SN14 22 B4
Wetherby Clo. SN14 22 A6
Whittle Clo. SN14 22 A4
Wicks Dri. SN15 23 F6
Willow Gro. SN15 23 E1
Willowbank. SN14 22 B2
Winchester Clo. SN14 23 E6
Windlass Way. SN15 23 F6
Windsor Clo. SN14 22 A5
Wishart Way. SN15 23 F6
Wood La. SN15 23 E5
Woodlands Rd. SN14 22 C4
Wyndham Clo. SN15 23 F3
Yewstock Cres East. SN15 22 C2
Yewstock Cres West. SN15 22 C2
York Clo. SN14 22 A5

CRICKLADE

Abingdon Ct La. SN6 26 C2
Bailiffs Peice. SN6 26 B1
Bath Ct. SN6 26 B2
Bath Rd. SN6 26 A2
Bishopsfields. SN6 26 A2
Branders. SN6 26 B1
Calcutt St. SN6 26 C2
Chelworth Rd. SN6 26 A3
Cherrytree Rd. SN6 26 A2
Church La. SN6 26 B2
Cirencester Rd. SN6 26 B1
Cliffords. SN6 26 A2
Common Hill. SN6 26 A2
Cricklade By-Pass. SN6 26 C1
Deansfield. SN6 26 B3
Doubledays. SN6 26 B2
Fairfield. SN6 26 B1
Fairview. SN6 26 C2
Fiddle Farm. SN6 26 A2
Foxleaze. SN6 26 B1
Fullers Av. SN6 26 C2
Galley Orchard. SN6 26 C2
Gas La. SN6 26 B2
Giles Av. SN6 26 B3
Hallsfield. SN6 26 A1
Hammonds. SN6 26 B2
High St. SN6 26 B2
Home Ground. SN6 26 A1
Hopkins Orchard. SN6 26 B3
Horse Fair La. SN6 26 C2
Keels. SN6 26 A1
Kitefield. SN6 26 B1
Lady Mead. SN6 26 A2
Malmesbury Rd. SN6 26 A2
Manor Orchard. SN6 26 C2
Middle Ground. SN6 26 A1
North Meadow Rd. SN6 26 A1
North Wall. SN6 26 B1
Ockwells. SN6 26 B3
Parsonage Farm Rd. SN6 26 B2
Pauls Croft. SN6 26 B3
Pike House Clo. SN6 26 A2

Pittsfield. SN6	26 B3
Pleydells. SN6	26 B1
Purton Rd. SN6	26 B3
Rectory La. SN6	26 C1
Red Lion La. SN6	26 C1
Reeds. SN6	26 A1
Saxon Clo. SN6	26 B2
Spital La. SN6	26 C2
Stones La. SN6	26 A4
Swindon Rd. SN6	26 C2
Thames Clo. SN6	26 C2
Thames La. SN6	26 C2
The Fiddle. SN6	26 A2
The Forty. SN6	26 B3
Water Furlong. SN6	26 B3
Waylands. SN6	26 B3
West Mill La. SN6	26 A1
White Horse Rd. SN6	26 B2

HIGHWORTH

Arran Way. SN6	4 A2
Barra Clo. SN6	4 A3
Biddel Springs. SN6	4 C3
Blandford Alley. SN6	4 B4
Botany. SN6	4 A1
Brewery St. SN6	4 C4
Brookfield. SN6	4 B2
Bute Clo. SN6	4 B2
Byde Mill Gdns. SN6	4 A4
Cherry Orchard. SN6	4 C3
Church Vw. SN6	4 B4
Crane Furlong. SN6	4 B2
Cricklade Rd. SN6	4 A4
Downs View. SN6	4 C3
Eastrop. SN6	4 C2
Edencroft. SN6	4 C2
Folly Clo. SN6	4 C2
Folly Cres. SN6	4 B2
Folly Dri. SN6	4 B2
Folly Way. SN6	4 C2
Grange Clo. SN6	4 C4
Grove Hill. SN6	4 B2
Grove Orchard. SN6	4 B2
Henley Dri. SN6	4 B2
High St. SN6	4 B2
Home Farm. SN6	4 A3
INDUSTRIAL ESTATES:	
Blackworth Ind Est. SN6	4 B1
Islay Cres. SN6	4 B3
Kilda Rd. SN6	4 A2
Kings Av. SN6	4 C4
Knowlands. SN6	4 C2
Lechlade Rd. SN6	4 B4
Lismore Rd. SN6	4 A2
Market Pl. SN6	4 C4
Middi Haines Ct. SN6	4 C3
Newburgh Pl. SN6	4 B3
North Vw. SN6	4 B4
Oak Dri. SN6	4 B4
Orange Clo. SN6	4 C3
Park Av. SN6	4 C4
Parsonage Ct. SN6	4 C4
Pentlands Clo. SN6	4 B2
Pentlands La. SN6	4 B1
Pound Rd. SN6	4 B2
Priory Grn. SN6	4 C3
Quarry Cres. SN6	4 B3
Queens Av. SN6	4 C2
Rivers Pl. SN6	4 B3
Roman Way. SN6	4 A4
Round Hills Mead. SN6	4 C1
St Michaels Av. SN6	4 A3
Sevenfields. SN6	4 C2
Sheep St. SN6	4 C4
Shrivenham Rd. SN6	4 C5
Skye Clo. SN6	4 A2
Spa Clo. SN6	4 C3
Stapleton Clo. SN6	4 B4
Station Rd. SN6	4 B4
Stonefields. SN6	4 B5
Stroma Way. SN6	4 A2
Swindon Rd. SN6	4 B6
Swindon St. SN6	4 C4
The Cullerns. SN6	4 C3
The Dormers. SN6	4 C3
The Elms. SN6	4 B4
The Green. SN6	4 B4
The Mews. SN6	4 C4
The Paddocks. SN6	4 C3
The Willows. SN6	4 C4
Turnpike Rd. SN6	4 C3
Vicarage La. SN6	4 B3
Vorda Rd. SN6	4 C2
Wessex Way. SN6	4 D2
Westhill Clo. SN6	4 B4
Westrop. SN6	4 B3
Windrush. SN6	4 A3
Wrde Hill. SN6	4 A4

MARLBOROUGH

Alexandra Ter. SN8	24 D2
Alma Pl. SN8	24 D3
Angel Yd. SN8	24 D3
Aubrey Clo. SN8	24 D3
Back La. SN8	24 C3
Bailey Acre. SN8	24 D3
Barn St. SN8	24 D3
Barnfield. SN8	25 G3
Barrow Clo. SN8	25 F3
Bath Rd. SN8	24 A4
Bay Water Vw. SN8	24 D2
Baybridge. SN8	25 F2
Benson Clo. SN8	24 D3
Betjeman Rd. SN8	24 A4
Blackwell Path. SN8	24 D3
Blowhorn St. SN8	24 D2
Bridewell St. SN8	24 C4
Bridge St. SN8	24 A4
Cardigan Rd. SN8	24 C3
Chantry La. SN8	24 D3
Cherry Orchard. SN8	25 E4
Chestnut Dri. SN8	24 D4
Chopping Knife La. SN8	25 G4
Cold Harbour La. SN8	24 D2
College Fields. SN8	24 B3
Copes Yd. SN8	25 E3
Cross La. SN8	24 C2
Culvermead Clo. SN8	25 E3
Dando Clo. SN8	24 B3
Davies Clo. SN8	24 A4
Ducks Meadow. SN8	24 D4
Edwards Mdw. SN8	24 D2
Elcot Clo. SN8	25 F3
Elcot La. SN8	25 F3
Elcot Orchard. SN8	25 G3
Falkner Clo. SN8	24 B3
Farrar Dri. SN8	24 A4
Figgins La. SN8	24 D4
Five Stiles Rd. SN8	25 F4
Forest Dale Rd. SN8	25 F3
Francklyn Acre. SN8	24 D2
Frees Av. SN8	24 B1
Gales Grd. SN8	25 E3
George La. SN8	24 A4
Golding Av. SN8	24 A4
Grand Av. SN8	25 H5
Granham Clo. SN8	24 C6
Granham Hill. SN8	24 C6
Hawkins Meadow. SN8	24 D4
Hazel Clo. SN8	25 G4
Herd St. SN8	24 D2
High St, Manton. SN8	24 A4
High St, Marlborough. SN8	24 D3
Hilliers Yd. SN8	24 D3
Homefields. SN8	25 F4
Hughenden Yd. SN8	24 D3
Hughes Clo. SN8	24 A4
Hyde La. SN8	24 C2
Ironmonger La. SN8	24 D3
Irving Clo. SN8	24 C3
Isbury La. SN8	24 D4
Isbury Rd. SN8	24 D4
Jefferies Clo. SN8	24 B4
Kennet Mews. SN8	24 D3
Kennet Pl. SN8	24 D3
Kingsbury St. SN8	24 D2
Lainey's Clo. SN8	25 F3
Laurel Dri. SN8	24 D4
Lawrence Acre. SN8	24 D2
Leaf Clo. SN8	25 E2
Leaze Rd. SN8	24 C2
London Rd. SN8	25 E3
Lower Church Fld. SN8	24 D4
Lyne's View. SN8	24 D4
MacNeice Dri. SN8	24 A3
Manton Drove. SN8	24 A6
Manton Hollow. SN8	24 A4
Mayfield. SN8	24 B4
Morris Rd. SN8	24 B4
New Rd. SN8	24 D3
Newby Acre. SN8	24 D2
North View Pl. SN8	24 D2
Orchard Rd. SN8	25 E4
Oxford St. SN8	24 D3
Pewsey Rd. SN8	24 D4
Plume of Feathers La. SN8	25 E3
Port Field. SN8	24 D2
Port Hill. SN8	24 D1
Poulton Cres. SN8	25 E2
Poulton Hill. SN8	25 E2
Preshute La. SN8	24 A4
Priorsfield. SN8	25 E4
Purlyn Acre. SN8	24 D2
Queens Way. SN8	25 E4
Rabley Wood Vw. SN8	24 D2
Ramsbury Rd. SN8	25 H2
Rawlings Well La. SN8	24 D3
Reeds Clo. SN8	25 F3
Reeds Cnr. SN8	25 F3
Riding School Yd. SN8	24 D4
River Park. SN8	24 D4
Roebuck Meadow. SN8	25 F3
Rogers Meadow. SN8	24 D1
Russel Sq. SN8	24 D2
St Davids Way. SN8	24 D2
St Johns Clo. SN8	24 C2
St Margarets Mead. SN8	25 E3
St Martins. SN8	24 D3
Salisbury Hill. SN8	25 E5
Salisbury Rd. SN8	25 E4
Sassoon Walk. SN8	24 B3
Savernake Ct. SN8	25 F4
Savernake Cres. SN8	25 F4
Shakespeare Dri. SN8	24 B3
Silverless St. SN8	24 D3
Sorley Clo. SN8	24 B3
South View. SN8	25 E2
Stonebridge Clo. SN8	25 E3
Stonebridge La. SN8	25 E3
Swindon Rd. SN8	24 D2
Tennyson Clo. SN8	24 B4
The Common. SN8	24 D2
The Green. SN8	24 D3
The Parade. SN8	24 D3
The Thorns. SN8	24 D1
Thomson Way. SN8	24 B4
Tinpit. SN8	25 E2
Town Mill. SN8	24 D3
Upper Church Fld. SN8	24 D4
Upper Isbury. SN8	24 D4
Van Diemans Clo. SN8	25 E4
Vicarage Clo. SN8	25 E3
Willow Clo. SN8	25 G3

WOOTTON BASSETT

Alderney Clo. SN4	12 D4
Arran Clo. SN4	12 D4
Aspen Clo. SN4	12 B3
Badger Clo. SN4	12 D4
Baileys Mead. SN4	12 D4
Bardsey Clo. SN4	12 D4
Bath Rd. SN4	12 A5
Beamans La. SN4	12 A4
Bennett Hill Clo. SN4	12 C4
Betjeman Av. SN4	12 C3
Binckoll La. SN4	12 C4
Blackthorn Clo. SN4	12 B2
Boroughfields. SN4	12 B4
Bradene Clo. SN4	12 C4
Branscombe Dri. SN4	12 C4
Briars Clo. SN4	12 B2
Brynards Hill. SN4	12 B5
Byron Av. SN4	12 C3
Chaucer Clo. SN4	12 C3
Church Hill Clo. SN4	12 D3
Church St. SN4	12 A4
Clarendon Dri. SN4	12 B4
Coleridge Clo. SN4	12 B3
Coxstalls. SN4	12 B4
Downs View. SN4	12 B4
Dryden Pl. SN4	12 C3
Dunnington Rd. SN4	12 B6
Eastwood Av. SN4	12 B4
Elm Clo. SN4	12 B2
Elm Park. SN4	12 B5
Englefield. SN4	12 B4
Everleigh Rd. SN4	12 B4
Fairfield. SN4	12 B3
Farne Way. SN4	12 D4
Fox Brook. SN4	12 C4
Gainsborough Av. SN4	12 C3
Garraways. SN4	12 D4
Glebe Rd. SN4	12 A5
Glenville Clo. SN4	12 B6
Goughs Way. SN4	12 C4
Hazel Rd. SN4	12 C5
High Mead. SN4	12 C4
High St. SN4	12 A5
Highfold. SN4	12 C5
Home Ground. SN4	12 D4
Homefield. SN4	12 C4
Honeyhill. SN4	12 B5
Horsell Clo. SN4	12 C4
Huntsland. SN4	12 C4
INDUSTRIAL ESTATES:	
Coped Hall Business Park. SN4	12 C2
Interface Business Centre. SN4	12 D4
Templars Way Ind Est. SN4	12 B6
Keats Clo. SN4	12 C3
Kingsley Av. SN4	12 B3
Laburnum Dri. SN4	12 B3
Lime Kiln. SN4	12 B3
Linden Clo. SN4	12 B2
Lindisfarne. SN4	12 D3
Longfellow Cres. SN4	12 C3
Longleaze. SN4	12 B3
Lucerne Clo. SN4	12 D4
Malmesbury Rd. SN4	12 A1
Maple Dri. SN4	12 B2
Marlborough Rd. SN4	12 B6
Marlowe Way. SN4	12 C3
Masefield. SN4	12 C3
Meadow Clo. SN4	12 B3
Middle Ground. SN4	12 D3
Miltons Way. SN4	12 A5
Morstone Rd. SN4	12 B5
New Rd. SN4	12 A5
Nore Marsh Rd. SN4	12 B5
Noredown Way. SN4	12 C4
Northbank Rise. SN4	12 C4
Old Court. SN4	12 B4
Old Malmesbury Rd. SN4	12 C2
Orchard Mead. SN4	12 D4
Otter Way. SN4	12 C4
Parhams Ct. SN4	12 C4
Parsons Way. SN4	12 B4
Pipers Clo. SN4	12 B5
*Potters Field, High St. SN4	12 A5
Queens Rd. SN4	12 B4
Ravens Walk. SN4	12 D3
Richards Clo. SN4	12 A5
Robins Clo. SN4	12 D3
Rope Yard. SN4	12 A4
Rowan Dri. SN4	12 C5
Ruskin Dri. SN4	12 C3
Ruxley Clo. SN4	12 C4
Rylands Way. SN4	12 B4
Saffron Clo. SN4	12 B2
Salt Spring Dri. SN4	12 C4
Shakespeare Rd. SN4	12 C3
Shelley Av. SN4	12 C3
Shepherds Breach. SN4	12 B4
Sherfields. SN4	12 C5
Sheridan Clo. SN4	12 C3
Showfield. SN4	12 B2
Skewbridge Clo. SN4	12 A5
Sorrell Clo. SN4	12 B2
Southbank Glen. SN4	12 C4
Springfield Cres. SN4	12 A3
Squires Hill Clo. SN4	12 C4
Squirrel Cres. SN4	12 C4
Station Rd. SN4	12 B4
Stoneover La. SN4	12 A5
Swallows Mead. SN4	12 B4
Swinburne Pl. SN4	12 C3
Swindon Rd. SN4	12 B3
Tanners Clo. SN4	12 B4
Templars Firs. SN4	12 B6
Templars Way. SN4	12 B6
Tennyson Rd. SN4	12 B4
The Burlongs. SN4	12 B4
The Lawns. SN4	12 A4
The Maltings. SN4	12 A5
The Mulberrys. SN4	12 B4
The Rosary. SN4	12 B4
The Steadings. SN4	12 B4
Tinkers Field. SN4	12 B4

Vale View. SN4	
Victory Row. SN4	
Vowley View. SN4	
Washbourne Rd. SN4	
Westbury Park. SN4	
Whitehill La. SN4	
Whitehorn Clo. SN4	
Withy Clo. SN4	
Wood St. SN4	
Woodshaw Mead. SN4	
Woolford Grange. SN4	
Wordsworth Clo. SN4	

WROUGHTON

Anthony Rd. SN4	
Artis Av. SN4	
Ashencope Rd. SN4	
Baileys Way. SN4	
Bakers Rd. SN4	
Barcelona Cres. SN4	
Barrett Way. SN4	
Beaufort Rd. SN4	
Berkeley Rd. SN4	
Bladen Clo. SN4	
Blenheim Rd. SN4	
Boness Rd. SN4	
Brettingham Gate. SN4	
Brimble Hill. SN4	
Burderop Clo. SN4	
Charter House Clo. SN4	
Church Hill. SN4	
Coombe Clo. SN4	
Coronation Rd. SN4	
Coventry Clo. SN4	
Cowleaze Cres. SN4	
Devizes Rd. SN4	
Dunbar Rd. SN4	
Edgar Row Clo. SN4	
Elcombe Av. SN4	
Ellingdon Rd. SN4	
Falkirk Way. SN4	
Greens La. SN4	
Hackpen Clo. SN4	
Halifax Clo. SN4	
Hall Clo. SN4	
Hicks Clo. SN4	
High St. SN4	
Hodson Rd. SN4	
Inverary Rd. SN4	
Kellsboro Av. SN4	
Kennet Rd. SN4	
Kerrs Way. SN4	
Lancaster Rd. SN4	
Lister Rd. SN4	
Manor Clo. SN4	
Markham Pl. SN4	
Markham Rd. SN4	
Marlborough Rd. SN4	
Marine Clo. SN4	
Maskeleyne Way. SN4	
Maunsell Way. SN4	
Mill Clo. SN4	
Moat Walk. SN4	
Moormead Rd. SN4	
Overtown Hill. SN4	
Perrys La. SN4	
Petter Clo. SN4	
Plummer Clo. SN4	
Priors Hill. SN4	
Purley Clo. SN4	
Roberts Clo. SN4	
St Andrews Clo. SN4	
St Andrews Ct. SN4	
St John Rd. SN4	
Savill Cres. SN4	
Snapps Clo. SN4	
Stirling Clo. SN4	
Summerhouse Rd. SN4	
Swindon Rd. SN4	
The Mountings. SN4	
The Pitchens. SN4	
Victoria Cross Rd. SN4	
Walley Cres. SN4	
Weirside Av. SN4	
Wharf Rd. SN4	
Willow Walk. SN4	
Woodland View. SN4	